Grievers Ask

Answers to Questions about Death and Loss

Harold Ivan Smith

Augsburg Books
MINNEAPOLIS

Grievers Ask is dedicated . . .

to the courageous individuals
who have participated in Grief Gatherings
and who have taught me from their experienced grief.
I owe a great debt of gratitude
for all that I have learned
from wise people on the grief path.

to Saint Luke's Hospital, Kansas City,
which has funded and facilitated the program,
and the nurses and chaplains
who have encouraged individuals to participate.

to Rhonda Monke
who does magic with manuscripts and asks,
"Are you sure you want to say that?"

GRIEVERS ASK
Answers to Questions about Death and Loss

This edition published in 2020 by Fortress Press, an imprint of 1517 Media.

Cover image: © iStock 2019; Dramatic clouds reflected in the water by Pobytov
Cover design: Alisha Lofgren

Print ISBN: 978-0-8066-4562-9
eBook ISBN: 978-1-4514-0945-1

Contents

Introduction

"All of us, though, have questions, longings,
and the challenge to reframe
who we are and what we believe
when we are bereaved."
—*Dick Gilbert*[1]

Sometimes you read particular words or notice a book title that you never forget. Like a squirrel preparing for winter, you hide the words for the night or dawn you will need them. My friend, Doug Manning, has written a book with the most intriguing title: *Don't Take My Grief Away*. The title alone is worth the price of the book, and inside it, Manning gives individuals permission to grieve and permission to have questions: "Eternity will have to last a long time," he writes. "I have enough questions to fill up a thousand years."[2]

Likewise, I have spent hours pondering and rehearsing my "whys." It is inevitable when you facilitate a program in which grievers gather around an unfinished Amish quilt to share their stories and voice tough questions. People of all kinds come to these Grief Gatherings. Wealthy and poor; young, older, and old; those who are talkative and those who are reserved; those who are faithful and those who do not believe, no longer believe, and are too angry to believe. All show up with questions.

For a time in my work, I thought I was supposed to "fix" grievers. I joined that cadre of professional helpers who have the goal of "getting 'em over it" or "getting 'em on with life." My goal was to guide the bereaved through the stages of grief to the destination—DONE! I listened to a question only long enough to summon a pre-packaged answer. Sometimes, I was unwilling to let the questioner get the entire question out. I assumed, from having listened to other grievers' questions or from my professional training, that I knew where this question was headed.

Questions are like icebergs. There is the visible, hearable part of the question, but lurking below the reality line is the deeper part of the question.

In the same way, many adults deny grief by dishing out clichés instead of pondering and "receiving" grievers' questions. In many languages, many dialects, grievers have heard, "Best not to dwell on it," "Get over it!" or "Someday God will make it plain." Underlying the latter is the belief that by the time "someday" rolls around the question will no longer matter.

Too many individuals distance themselves from the questioning process with a "Don't go there!" approach. Sometimes a look or a tone of voice discourages a question. Even those who deal professionally with dying, death, and bereavement may have a fear of death that shapes or limits their openness and their answers. A professional credential does not bestow immunity from death fears. Grievers quickly learn the consequences of a premature question or a question that makes a comforter uncomfortable. Grievers learn that some family and friends—even pastors and counselors—have an informal "statute of limitations" on questioning and on grieving. They learn that listeners communicate discomfort in a multitude of ways.

Grievers taught me that my responsibility is to provide an environment in which grievers feel safe voicing questions. My task is to "receive" the questions, to offer hospitality to the questioner.

Some grievers wait until they are certain a Grief Gathering is a safe place to unleash powerful questions. These questions can suck the air out of a room. More than once after a particular disclosure, I have instructed participants, "Take a deep breath with me." Sometimes, the question-asker does not expect an answer. Just asking can comfort. For others, comfort comes in discovering they are not the first to ask the question.

Grievers Ask is a compilation of common questions grievers voice. A question asked at any Monday night gathering—whether on a snowy February night, a balmy May night, a sizzling August night, or a "winter-is-coming" October night—may have been asked a dozen, a hundred, or a thousand years earlier by a griever whose loss was as devastating or as puzzling. Kings and serfs, princesses and milkmaids, archbishops and parishioners, generals and privates, masters and slaves, tycoons and servants, managers and laborers have asked questions identical to or similar to those in this book. Some grievers have offered wealth or fame to anyone who could come up with a satisfactory answer. Some have, for a moment or a day or a year, thought they had the answer, only to see it burst like a bubble in the wind.

Some grievers feel punished by their loss. "I don't know *why* such a great price was exacted for occupying the White House," President Calvin Coolidge groaned after the death of his sixteen-year-old son, Calvin Jr., from blood poisoning in July 1924.[3] None of his presidential advisers or aides was able to draft a suitable answer. Pondering his "whys," the president often stared out the Oval Office window to the tennis court where he had seen his son play so many afternoons.

For many, the question is, "Now what?" or "How do I live without . . . ?" Some whys are not about the death but about a disclosure after the death. In April 1945, Eleanor Roosevelt flew to Warm Springs, Georgia, to accompany the body of her husband, President Franklin Delano Roosevelt, back to the White House. In asking questions for clarification about his death, she discovered the president had not been alone when he died. Lucy Mercer Rutherford—whom Eleanor assumed Franklin had given up when she discovered the relationship in 1918—had been with him for three days. Through a long night on the funeral train, Eleanor remained awake pondering her whys. Why had their daughter, Anna, helped arrange the meetings? Why had Secret Service agents become involved in the deception? Who else knew about the relationship? By the time Eleanor reached the White House, she had a mile-long list of whys. She was not thinking about what her future held.

When reporters asked her what was next, the new widow replied, "The story is over." Elsewhere, President Harry Truman was mulling over his "what nexts" and chose to appoint her to the U.S. delegation to the formation of the United Nations. What Eleanor could not have imagined were the years ahead as a distinguished diplomat, humanitarian, and advocate for women.

Every griever's question deserves to be honored. Questions are not only important for the answers, but questions are also ways to ponder the great mystery of life that most people want to dodge: death.

I always learn from the questions grievers ask about dying, death, and bereavement. More than once I have had to admit that any answer was less than adequate, or that I was struggling with the question, too. I have always tried to respect the dignity of every questioner, especially those trying to balance an enormous load of grief that I have never experienced.

Some questions have jarred me. Some questions sneak back into my mind during showers or walking along a beach or trying to fall back to sleep at three AM. Some questions have sent me to libraries to find answers; others have sent me to colleagues, asking, "How would you answer this question?" Some questions have led me to a griever farther down the trail who has lived into an answer.

Grievers sometimes ask me questions, not because they think I will know the answer but rather because they find me open to their questions. I think grievers ask questions, paraphrasing C. S. Lewis, to know they are not alone in their wonderings about the ironies and paradoxes, timing and outrages of loss. At times, all I can offer is hospitality to question-bearers.

Hopefully, you will find *Grievers Ask* an invitation to voice your questions. You will find some of your questions rephrased in the questions in this book. Some of the critical questions have not been "niced up." They are raw, experience-shaped questions forged in the depths of a particular loss. Some questions have been punctuated with multiple exclamation marks. Some questions do a soul good for the asking. Some questions are "just itching" to be asked.

Some of the answers may not meet your litmus test of satisfaction or sensitivity. You may even scoff at some answer, "*What!* He doesn't get it!" Still, in these answers you may find raw material from which you can create answers. Or you may find a seedling that will become, over time, the answer.

Don't let anyone take your questions away from you.

Sometimes grievers meander their ways into answers. Grievers work a potential answer the way artists work with a lump of clay. And grievers revisit answers that initially satisfied them.

Give yourself permission to ask your questions. You can start anywhere in *Grievers Ask*. Pick a section that interests you and begin reading. Hopefully, somewhere in *Grievers Ask* you will find the particle of sand that gets trapped in the oyster shell, which over time becomes a pearl.

If you do not find answers, keep asking. Be open to "answers" coming from unexpected sources. That's why Southerners have so commonly sung at funerals, "We will understand it better by and by." The answer to today's question may come in another's experience of loss. Many grievers also "live" their way into answers.

Someday you may, from tending your experience, become the answer to another griever's question. Plato said the unexamined life is not worth living. Well, an unquestioned grief is not worth experiencing.

Be cautious of easy answers that come packaged with neatness and overconfidence and smiles. Never let anyone dodge the question or pat you on the head with the equivalent of, "There, there." Former baseball great Dave Dravecky observed: "There is no such thing as a bad question. The issue is not with the questions, or even how we ask them. The issue is where we go with questions. Any question that brings us to God for an answer is a good question."[4]

The great tragedies are *unasked* questions. Had a griever asked, or continued to ask, you might already have an answer you need—an answer that becomes the life raft in the stormy seas of grief.

Give *your* questions a voice.

1. Questions about the Duration of Grief

"There may be one-minute managers,
but there are no one-minute mourners."
—*Ellen Goldman*[1]

"You may be coming to understand one
of the fundamental truths of grief:
Your journey will never end.
People do not 'get over' grief. . . .
We are forever changed by the experience of grief."
—*Alan D. Wolfelt*[2]

"The mourning clock ticks at many speeds
and without rules."
—*Carol Fredericks Ebeling*[3]

Q1. How long should it take to get over a death?

It depends. Grief is an individualized experience of a particular
loss of a particular relationship. Suppose a mother of three adult
children dies after a battle with cancer. Biologically the siblings

had the same mother, but emotionally and relationally they had different experiences. The mother may have been closer to one child; she may have had a favorite (or a child may have assumed Mom had a favorite). One of the children may have been more of a caretaker during the mother's illness. Moreover, some of the siblings may have anticipated the death; they may have been doing anticipatory grieving since the diagnosis or since the reoccurrence of a disease. These siblings may assume they had a head start on "getting over" the death.

It takes as long as it takes. Grief theorist J. William Worden cautions, "Asking when mourning is finished is a little like asking how high is up." He explains further:

> One benchmark of a completed grief reaction is when the person is able to think of the deceased without pain. There is always a sense of sadness when you think of someone that you have loved and lost, but it is a different kind of sadness— it lacks the wrenching quality it previously had.[1]

Carol Fredericks Ebeling, from her long experience in hospice care, offers four "mile markers" that help grievers determine their progress toward integrating the loss:

The griever uses the hard words for death. Rather than use a euphemism such as "My child is gone," the griever says straightforwardly, "My child *died*."

The griever talks about the loss without being overwhelmed by tears.

The griever can feel good about feeling good.

The griever can risk change. Statements such as "He wouldn't want me to . . ." or "She would want me to . . ." do not bind the griever.[2]

Richard Obershaw, director of The Grief Center, would say the answer is based on your responses to three questions:

What have I lost?

How do I feel about it?

Who am I now without _____?[3]

Take a moment and think about those three questions. Remember there are "secondary" losses as well. The loss of a second income, the loss of the partner who "managed" the investments, the loss of the parent who was the disciplinarian—these gaps can greatly complicate your grief.

Q2   My friends say I should be over my grief by now. What do I say to them?

You are grieving your loss in a "get-over-it," "move-on-with-it" world. Many individuals assume a grief should last about thirty days. Some of your friends may have never experienced the death of a close family member; they have no real understanding of what you are experiencing. Focus on your grief. In the future, when your friends experience grief, as they will, your example of taking as much time as you need to work through your grief will encourage them to do the same.

With some friends you may have to be direct, saying: "Let me tell you how the idea that I should 'be over it by now' sounds to me." In fact, you may be doing them a big favor by having a straightforward conversation with them, so they realize how their words affect others.

Q3   Five years after our son's death my wife still cries. Is this normal?

In grief there is no "normal." Normal is a city in southern Illinois and a setting on a dryer. After a death, there is no getting back to "normal." Over time, if you cooperate with grief, a new "normal" emerges. The process of grieving is never finished, although our culture does its best to rush grievers through their grief. Moreover, a death must be revisited at key developmental stages or milestones. For example, a six-year-old girl who lost her mother will have to deal with that loss again when she begins menstruating and there's no mom to talk to. Or when she graduates and there is no mom snapping pictures. Or at her wedding, when there is no mother of the bride. Or when she has her first child and there is no "Grandma" to call in the middle of the night with a "What do I do?" question. Admittedly, there may be a stepmom but, for many, it is not the same.

Dwight D. Eisenhower's three-year-old son, Izzy, died in 1921. A World War II general and two-term president, he never "got over" his son's death, calling it "the greatest disappointment and disaster in my life . . . the one I have never been able to forget completely."[1]

Sometimes, grief re-announces itself around anniversaries. That is why the Jews have wisely created *yahrzeit*—the recognition of the anniversary of a death. It is a way of acknowledging and memorializing the person by saying, "Nine (or whatever number) years ago today (my son, my mother, my best friend) died."

Q4 Will I have to live with this pain for the rest of my life?

My friend, whose eighteen-year-old son died thirteen years ago, concluded, "It doesn't get better—it gets different." The pain will change. Early in a particular grief, the pain and confusion dominate. But if you "dance" with the pain and pay attention to it, you will learn to live with the pain.

The real question is what will you do with the pain. "God's role," according to Harold Kushner, "is not to protect us from pain and loss, but to protect us from letting pain and loss define our lives."[1]

Some grievers have used pain to do amazing things. Candice Lightener and other mothers who had their children die in incidents involving drunk drivers organized MADD—Mothers Against Drunk Drivers—in 1980. They used pain to make a difference in public awareness and in challenging drinking-and-driving laws in the United States. After their only son died, the Leland Stanford family used the pain to create the Leland Stanford Junior University. Dee and Vincent Ragusa took their pain and turned their car into a rolling memorial to their son, Michael, a fireman, who died in the World Trade Center collapse. On the hood is their son's name, a large facsimile of his badge, and the words, "Forever in our hearts."[2]

Some grievers volunteer for civic organizations, create scrapbooks, or share mementos with friends. Others work tirelessly for changes, such as getting a traffic light or stop sign installed at a dangerous intersection. There are lots of ways to use the pain and lessons learned in grief for the good.

Q5　How much credence should I give to the "stages" of grief?

None. The so-called stages of grief—denial, anger, bargaining, depression, and acceptance (or some variation on those five)—was popularized in the 1970s and 1980s by the Swiss psychiatrist Elisabeth Kübler-Ross as an explanation for emotions experienced during the dying process. Over time, others hijacked the theory and began applying it to bereavement and to every other imaginable type of loss.

Kübler-Ross's study was composed entirely of volunteers and is, by its methodology, flawed. To her credit, Kübler-Ross helped society find its voice to talk about death, dying, and grieving issues. However, many of the nation's top thanatologists (specialists in grief counseling and grief education) believe the theory has significant limitations because of the way it has been misinterpreted. Robert Neimeyer, of the University of Memphis, rejects the stages, saying, "I no longer assume that people experience a universal sequence of stages or tasks following the loss or that the process of grieving can usefully be viewed as eventuating in an end state of 'recovery.'"[1] He adds:

As human beings struggling with seemingly inhuman demands, we all too often find ourselves caricatured in the overly simple portrayal of grief offered by traditional "stage" theories of adaptation to loss. Not only do these theories seem strangely anonymous in their description of supposedly universal symptoms of grief and phases of emotional reactions, but they also seem to miss the particulars of our struggle, and its embeddedness in a life that is uniquely our own.[2]

Too many grief specialists have taken Kübler-Ross's material and created a "one-size-fits-all" template without seriously examining the groundwork on which her concept is based or the particularities of the grief to which they are applying the theory.

For some grievers, the stages of grief are something they can initially hang on, to try to understand or explain the unexplainable. But my objection is that stages are perceived to be a linear progression to "get over it" and "get back to normal." The stages overlook the incredible differences between grievers grieving the same individual. Stages encourage passive rather than responsive decision making.

Q6 How can I know whether I am "doing" the stages of grief correctly?

Sinatra may have been right when he crooned, "I did it my way." You may want to modify his words to sing, "I did grief my way." Too many people have turned the stages of grief from a theory into a litmus test to evaluate a griever's progress. "You should be in this stage by now."

Give your grief time. No two grievers follow the same path, even for the same loved one or the same type of loss. What is your heart telling you? I like the way Ellen Goodman expressed the reality, "In real lives, grief is a train that doesn't run on anyone else's schedule."[1]

Q7   Is there another way to conceptualize grief other than "stages of grief"?

Many grievers believe an individual has to cooperate with the grieving process. Grief is not a tame river you "float" through on a rafting expedition. It can be a wild river with lots of rapids that can be distressing and dangerous.

William Worden suggests "tasks" as an alternative concept. Tasks are more active. You probably have a "to do" list for this week, or maybe you make a list of the things you need to complete before you leave on vacation. In grieving, tasks are "opportunities" for engaging and integrating the loss. Worden identifies four tasks that grievers must respond to:

1. To accept the reality of the loss
2. To work through *to* the pain of the loss
3. To adjust to environments in which the person is missing
4. To "relocate" and memorialize the loved one[1]

Such tasks, however helpful, must not be seen as the only way to understand grief or the definitive replacement of the stages.

Some grievers try to "dodge" the first task by pretending the individual is not dead but perhaps away on a trip. A death can be more difficult to process if you saw the individual only occasionally or once a year. This reality complicates grief for children whose grandparents lived thousands of miles away or visited infrequently. But sooner or later a griever has to accept the reality of the loss: my loved one *died*.

In the second task, grievers have to work through *to* the pain—those incredible moments when the feeling of missing someone paralyzes us with an intensity we never imagined possible. When tears are not spilled, they seek revenge somewhere in the body. The emotional pain sometimes translates into physical pain in order to gain our attention. Few grievers have sufficient vocabulary to wrap around loss in order to explain it adequately. But they gain perspective while trying to assemble the words to package the loss.

Grievers must adjust to environments in which the person is missing. Specific moments and environments can ambush grievers. Some find their loss unbearable at mealtime or bedtime when the grief whispers (or shouts) "I'm back!" One mother, grieving for a child, shared, "Bedtime was our special time—just the two of us." Painful environments may be bedrooms—one previously shared with a spouse or a child's room now empty—or dining rooms, where one less place setting is needed for a family holiday dinner. Facing the loss in those environments is an emotional gain; it would be far easier to avoid them. Grievers may pray, "God, help me in this place. . . ."

Grievers need to work through to the pain of the loss. Grief can be outrageously painful. An impatient culture misreads this task as "to work through the pain of the loss." In other words, to get over it ASAP.

The fourth task is to relocate and memorialize the deceased. Many grapple with the question "Where is my loved one *now*?" Many, for example, find great comfort in the belief in heaven. Gordon Walker lost a newborn and his father within a matter of hours. The shock of the baby's death was too much for a grandfather-to-be who was "'hanging on' to see his soon-expected great-grandbaby." Walker considered this a "double-portion" loss. In time, however, Walker found comfort in "the assurance that my father was the first member of our family to see and enjoy Nathaniel James" in heaven.[2] Not everyone has such a belief.

Tony Walter contends, "The purpose of grief is not to move on without these who have died, but to find a secure place for them."[3] For some grievers, this is realized through storing up memories or stories about their loved one, or through commitments to support their values or philanthropies. Some people find security in a grave. Michael Regusa was the last of the 343 New York firefighters to be ritualized. His parents waited for two years for "something" to bury. Then the Regusas discovered that Michael, along with a group of his fellow firefighters, had volunteered to be a bone marrow donor and had given a blood sample. On his birthday, Michael's parents received a two-inch vial of his blood and made plans for their son's funeral. His mother explained, "If he's not laid to rest, it's like he never was. I want something that marks that he was alive. It makes him real. It says he was."[4]

Q8   Someone told me I need to do grief work. What is "grief work?"

Grief work means paying close attention to grief. Grief work is the necessary psychological and spiritual energy you must expend to integrate the loss—or this latest loss—into the story of your life. Charlotte Zillinger said it well: "If a grief is not used, it is wasted."[1] She learned that reality after her daughter was murdered.

Grief work focuses on a simple question, "Now what?" Or to restate: "What do I do with the life I have left to live?" Or "How do I live meaningfully without (name)?" Grief work is about reflection, journaling, and prayerful conversation with God about the future—a future that has been altered without your permission. Grief work is about participating in grief groups and learning from the experience of others. Grief work is talking about your feelings with a bereavement counselor. Grief work is *not* about "getting over it and moving on with life"!

Many people want to do something "about" their grief. The wiser guidance is, "Do something *with* your grief."

Q9 What is grief recovery?

We often use the word "recovery" as a financial or a medical term: You recover from a bankruptcy or a plunge in the value of your stock portfolio. You recover from an accident, from a trauma, from a heart attack, or from a bowel obstruction. But you do not recover from a death.

For many in this culture, "grief recovery" is a polite euphemism for "getting over it." Used in this sense, the term is a clichéd oxymoron that most grievers are too polite to challenge. Over the last two decades, grief has become increasingly medicalized. Adults often turn first to a physician for help. One hundred years ago, a griever would have sought out a minister, priest, or rabbi.

I do not believe in recovery from a death as in the euphemism "grief recovery." I believe grief recovery is a process and an expectation. I agree with Bruce Vaughn, who says, "What we need today is not 'grief recovery,' but *the recovery of grief*, meaning not recovery *from* grief, but the recovery *of* grief."[1] He defines grief as "a process in which we learn how to go on loving someone who is no longer there."[2]

Q10 Is it advisable to "keep busy" and to get back to a lot of activities?

In January 2001, Jean Carnahan, from Missouri, was appointed to fill the senate seat her deceased husband, Mel, won in 2000. A plane crash had killed not only her husband but also a son and a close family friend and aide. Senator Joseph Biden of Delaware approached his new colleague at the well of the senate chamber after she was sworn in. He offered this advice, "Work, hard work. It's the sure path to healing." Biden had a keen experience of grief; his first wife had been killed in a small plane crash on election night in 1972 when he won the Senate seat.[1]

Variations on this advice are being offered to thousands of grievers as you read this book. "Back to work" is something of a litmus test, the assumed proof of a completed, "successful" grief. Some of the most common advice mumbled in funeral homes is, "Stay busy!" Unfortunately, many grievers use work and activities as a way of dodging the pain of grief.

Grief, however, has ways to get your attention—your full attention. Give yourself and others in the family repeated permission to ignore the advice to "keep busy."

2. Questions about Asking Why

"When Jesus addressed God for the final time,
he no longer presumes to use the language
of filial intimacy. He uses no words of his own at all
but only a desperately recalled verse
from the Hebrew psalm,
'My God, my God, why have you forsaken me?'
That's surely as desolate a dying cry
as any thoughtful creature ever uttered."
—*Reynolds Price*[1]

"Long ago Barbara and I lost a tiny four-year-old girl
to leukemia. Of course we felt she was the most beautiful,
wonderful little girl that God had ever put on this earth.
We kept saying, 'Why? Why our Robin?
Why our gentle child of smiles and innocence?'
Lots of people tried to help us find the answer."
—*George H. Bush*[2]

Q11   My father-in-law says it is not for us to ask why? So what am I to do with my "whys"?

Spouses or parents do not always respond in tandem to the death of a child, nor siblings to the death of a parent. One parent may, in deep pain, want to get over it and "move on," perhaps because she or he cannot imagine living with such grief. The other parent wants to come to some logical "I-can-live-with" understanding of why the child died.

Some co-grievers decide early on that nothing they say, do, or think can bring back a loved one. So, in a modification of the adage, "You can't cry over spilled milk" they pull up the drawbridge on questions.

On the other hand, some grievers will accept any explanation. A bad explanation is better than no explanation. Bennie Pierce, age eleven, was decapitated in a train accident shortly before his father, Franklin Pierce, became president of the United States in 1853. Initially, Jane Pierce concluded that God had "taken" her son so her husband "could focus on his duties as president without distraction."[1] Franklin Pierce had repeatedly told his wife he had not wanted the presidential nomination. Later Jane learned from a cousin, Senator Charles Atherton, that her husband had actively sought the presidency. She concluded that God had "taken" Bennie to punish the president for lying to her. While Jane's aunt, Abby Kent

Grappling with "why" questions are the heart of the hard work of grief.

Means, served as the official hostess in the White House, Jane spent her days upstairs writing letters to her dead son.[2]

Never be in a hurry to formulate or settle on an answer to a "why?" For some grievers a "why" path leads down an uncomfortable-but-necessary trail, particularly in the cases of wrongful death or homicide: "Why did they have to kill her?"

From a spiritual perspective, "why" questions can be puzzling or troubling to those who stand on the margins of our grief. I have long wondered why a Vanderbilt University professor went in for surgery on a broken ankle and died. I have wondered why a twenty-nine-year-old physician—who had just finished her residency and had opened a practice in a community that desperately needed a physician—died in an automobile collision on a rural road. I have wondered why an eighteen-year-old named Mark with a brilliant future ahead of him died three days after high school graduation. You grieve in a culture that has lost its ability or willingness to ponder mysteries, preferring instead sound bites and easy answers—even when knowing there is little substance to the answer.

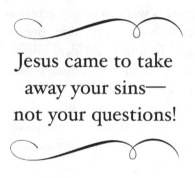

Jesus came to take away your sins— not your questions!

Individuals labeled by Tony Walter as the "grief police" take it upon themselves to go around extinguishing such questions. "It is not for us to ask 'why.'" Really?

It is sometimes hard to have a relationship with God in a world where such outrageous things happen. The unexplainables lead some to become part-time atheists.

I have long valued the assessment of Frederica Mathewes-Green: "The only useful question in such a time is not 'Why?' but 'What's next?' What should I do next? What should be my response to this ugly event? How can I bring the best out of it? How can God bring Resurrection out of it?"[3] To this list, I would add one question, "How can I partner with God to bring meaning out of this significant loss?" Some individuals will never find an acceptable answer to a "why" question. But about 99.9 percent of the time you will find an acceptable answer to a "now what" question.

Bring your "why" questions to a journal. Bring your "why" questions to a counselor or to a support group. Bring your "why" questions to God. Joseph Scovern, who experienced the deaths of two fiancées, wrote the gospel song, "What a Friend We Have in Jesus." Scovern reminds us:

"Oh, what peace we often forfeit

Oh, what needless pain we bear.

All because we do not carry

Everything to God in prayer."[4]

"Everything" in this song includes every "why" and "WHY!!!" you have.

Q12 My eighty-two-year-old mother is in ill health. She asks, "Why is the Lord keeping me alive? What do I have to live for?" What do I say to her?

Why is a man alive at ninety-five while his five-year-old great-grandson is struck and killed by a car when he chases a ball into the street? Death is a mystery. You can go to an observatory, look into the night sky, and name the stars or comets. You can go into a laboratory and identify tiny microorganisms that cannot be seen with the naked eye. You can trust a computer's answer to complex mathematical dilemmas. But despite all our sophistication, death remains a mystery. Sit in a specialist's waiting room and notice two patients, same age, similar circumstances with the same diagnosis and treatment plan. Yet, in twelve months, one is dead and one is in remission, if not healthy. Why?

With regard to your mother, one may ask, "What possible purpose does God have in prolonging this life?" The psalmist pondered a question very similar to this and wrote: "The Lord will fulfill his purpose for me; your love, O Lord, endures forever—do not abandon the works of your hands" (Psalm 138:8).

God may keep a person alive for a birthday, wedding, anniversary, graduation, or some other special occasion. God may keep someone alive in order to participate in the clinical trials for a new drug or treatment. God may keep an individual alive as something of a "witness" to a physician. Dr. Sherwood Nuland took the incredible lessons in courage that he learned from terminally ill patients and turned them into a best-seller, *How We Die*. God may keep someone alive until the individual is convinced that "unfinished business" is finished. Many believers find comfort in the example of God giving fifteen years to King Hezekiah (see 2 Kings 20:1-6).

The last part of your mother's question is the most important part: "What do I have to live for?" Keep talking to your elderly parents. I worry about families that do not talk during this critical experience called dying. Talk even if it is difficult or draining. Invite God to be present in the conversations. Breathe a brief prayer: "Be present in this conversation, O Lord," or "God, guide our conversation," or "God bring us insight, comfort, and peace in these conversations." Turn the question around and ask your parent, "Why do *you* think the Lord is keeping you alive?"

Questions do not always have answers, especially questions about death and dying. But asking and pondering questions strengthen relationships.

I find great meaning in these words, "For when David had served God's purpose in his own generation, he fell asleep" (Acts 13:36).

Q13 How do I respond when a griever says, "I have nothing to live for now that (name) is gone"?

Sometimes, there is nothing you can say that can take away the despair. But the statement is an invitation for you to be with this individual, perhaps to hold a hand and listen, perhaps to sit in silence with the individual, especially when others have fled or dished out spiritualized clichés.

Some individuals are physically and emotionally fatigued after serving as caregivers to a parent, spouse, or child. Some so invest their lives in their roles as spouses or parents, they cannot imagine life without a loved one. Many individuals through history have felt this way. Jacqueline Kennedy, soon after the president's assassination, told a priest she was contemplating suicide. Those were not idle words. She informed close friends, "I consider my life to be over, and I will spend the rest of it waiting for it really to be over."[1] On another occasion, she told Dr. Max Jacobson, "My life is over, Max. Just empty, meaningless." Jacobson laboriously tried to convince her "that there were many important things she could do in the future." He reminded her of her earlier work as a journalist and her interests in art and historical restoration. "I tried my best to impress upon her that life would go on, eventually, and the sooner she realized it, the better it would be."[2] One wise priest, Father Richard McSorley, simply listened to her lament.

Listen and be with a griever who needs you. If you feel comfortable you might say something to this effect, "Whenever I pray for you, I am going to ask God to give you a reason to live."

3. Questions about Remembering

"I'm convinced the reason we are here is to remember,
if we understand memory to be that uniquely human ability
to create from the past a sense of meaning in the present
and a trembling anticipation of possibility for the future."
—*A student to Elizabeth Harper Neeld*[1]

"Nostalgia is sweet because we focus not on our deprivation
but instead on how good it was when our loved one
was alive. The nostalgia comforts us.
But it is merely a temporary respite
from present concerns."
—*Thomas Attig*[2]

"Remembering is an act of resurrection,
each repetition a vital layer of mourning,
in memory of those we are sure to meet again."
—*Nancy Cobb*[3]

Q14　Does "moving on" mean I have to forget my spouse? We were soon to celebrate twenty-five years together.

In a "get-over-it" and "move-on-with life" culture, some individuals pick up the idea they have to stop loving a "loved one." Thomas Attig, a philosopher who has written extensively on death, disagrees. "Grieving is a journey that teaches us how to love in a new way now that our loved one is no longer with us. Consciously remembering those who have died is the key that opens our hearts, that allows us to love them in new ways."[1]

Remembering is a way of "making meaning" of a life. Tony Walter insists, "The last chapter is written after death by the survivors as they too go over the life lived and, separately or together, make sense of it." While there are public opportunities, such as eulogies, where we sometimes share that meaning with others, "often it is informally constructed between friends and family members."[2] All it takes is the question, "Do you remember the time . . . ?"

One of the last admonitions Jesus gave to his disciples was "Remember me." In fact, those words have been embedded in the communion invitation: "Do this, whenever you drink it, in remembrance of me" (1 Corinthians 11:25).

This poem has meaning for me:

As you died, I cried,
words impotent in such a moment.
I asked only one question, "What can I do?"
"Remember me," you whispered.
I am remembering you.[3]

Q15 Some friends say I should stop talking so much about my loved one and get on with my life. I do not want to forget. Do I have to stop remembering? Do I have a right to remember him?

You have not only a right to remember, but also an obligation. Carol Frederick Ebeling explains why it is important to talk about loss, "Each time the story is told, a little more pain is squeezed out, and the need to talk about the details decreases."[1]

Lots of individuals committed to great causes die young. Martin Luther King Jr. died at the age of thirty-nine; he did not get to the "promised land" of racial justice he envisioned. However, the message of Dr. King in many ways is stronger now than it was in April 1968, even though after his death some thought, "There, that will shut him up." His widow, Coretta Scott King, committed herself to raising their children and to launching the Martin Luther King Jr. Center for Nonviolent Social Change in Atlanta. Every day for more than thirty-five years she has been surrounded by memories of her husband; she has helped a new generation remember his message of nonviolence and contemplate his vision for racial harmony.

When you remember someone publicly, you give permission to others to remember with you. You also model a healthy dimension of grief that others will need to know about when their grief season comes.

Three grief researchers and authors, Dennis Klass, Phyllis R. Silverman, and Steven L. Nickman, have helped grievers understand a wonderful mystery they label "continuing bonds."[2] They challenge the cultural imperative to sever the relationships and urge grievers to make room for their loved ones and ancestors in their hearts and find ways to build bridges to their lives.

In many ethnic traditions there is a particular time for remembering the ancestors, like Day of the Dead among Hispanics, Memory Day among Vietnamese. The Jewish practice of *yizkor*, or prayers of remembrance, encourages building connections to those who have died. By reciting these prayers on Yom Kippur and other Jewish holidays, synagogues offer remembrance services that "continue the bonds." Harold Kushner writes,

> That is why the Jewish calendar asks us to pause five times a year, on the four holiday seasons and on the anniversary of a death, to remember those whom we have loved and lost. It is a way of giving us permission to go on with our lives without having to fear that we will forget, that we will leave precious but painful memories behind.[3]

Remember to remember. And remember to remember realistically: the good, the bad, and, unfortunately, the ugly.

Q16 What about the adage, "Speak no ill of the dead"?

It is essential, according to noted grief therapist, Therese Rando, to "remember realistically."[1] Sometimes, in bowing to the cultural admonition "speak no ill of the dead," individuals fail to grieve the real person and create a fictionalized loved one. Some families collude to create a "scripted" reality. Our mind, however, knows what the real person was like.

Some grievers work hard to "airbrush" personalities and relational histories. My friend Frank Freed, in his years as a therapist, asked clients, "What are you pretending not to know?" I borrow the phrase and ask, "What are you pretending not to know *about the deceased*?" Or "What are you pretending not to know *about your relationship with the deceased*?" Or to put it another way, "What do you *not* miss?"

May it be the real you who remembers the real deceased.

Jennifer Elison and Chris McGonigle, in their silence-shattering book, *Liberating Losses*, remind grievers that not all deceased individuals qualify as "loved ones." Even the phrase "loved one" keeps some grievers from acknowledging the real relationship.[2]

It must be admitted that we may have had a different or difficult relationship with a deceased parent, sibling, or child. This is one reason every effort should be made to deal with unfinished business before a death. But, in reality, some of us are not able to resolve all existing issues. So, we do postmortem resolution. This is particularly important work for those who have been recipients of physical, verbal, or sexual abuse.

The Jews have long practiced *hesped*, the balanced eulogy: pluses and minuses. An Orthodox Jewish saying goes, "Cursed be anyone who says 'Amen,' to a false eulogy." Some individuals and families must do hard grief work to construct what Denman Dewey called a "cherishable memory."[3] While some have lavish, cherished memories, others have only meager molecules. But those molecules, like seeds, if tended, over time can grow into a comforting memory.

Sometimes, grievers have to let the real life speak for itself.

Q17 Some individuals are uncomfortable when I mention my dead son's name. Should I stop saying his name?

"From this point on, pronoun!" is a message sometimes communicated to the grieving. I suspect you believe, especially now, that your son's name is beautiful. People around you, however, fear saying the name will cause you to feel sad or depressed. Actually, what makes you sad is when friends start relying on the pronoun "he" or "she," or on titles such as "your son," to avoid saying the name.

I would urge you to let it be their problem. Say your son's name. When you say his name—and demonstrate that you are comfortable with saying and hearing his name—you give others permission to say his name.

I find it fascinating that the Leland Stanford family, after the death of Leland Jr., chose to name a university after him. Their son's name is on every sheepskin: The Leland Stanford *Junior* University. You may not be able to endow a university in the name of your loved one, but you can, at every opportunity, say the name with no hint of apology. An individual may be dead but she is not "dead *and gone*" until we stop saying the name and stop telling stories about her.

4. Questions about Regrets

"In order to deal with unfinished business,
we must first honestly acknowledge
that we are troubled about how things
were between us and we need to identify
specifically what troubles us."
—*Thomas Attig*[1]

Q18 Although I try to focus on the positives in
my marriage, I seem to remember the
unpleasant. I was not always a good husband.
What do I do with my regrets?

One issue that complicates grief work is sticking rigorously to a memorialization. The Pope is not the only one who can make a saint. It's little wonder that some people become uncomfortable during funeral eulogies and homilies. We need to remember our loved ones had two sides just as we grievers have two sides: the public side and the private side. How do we acknowledge some of the hidden realities?

In the film *The Mission*, the hero had killed his brother after catching him in bed with his fiancée. As a punishment to remind him of his action, he had to drag around a huge bag of metal objects.

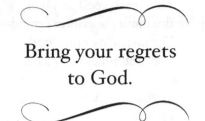

Bring your regrets to God.

As the monks and this man were tackling a steep, slippery slope in the South American jungle, he was having difficulty climbing with the weight. Finally, an Indian took a knife and cut the rope and let the bundle tumble into the roaring river below. There erupted the most incredible scene of joy I have ever seen in a movie.

Here are some suggestions for dealing with regrets:

～ Use this prayer fragment from *The Book of Common Prayer*, "'Almighty God, to you all hearts are open, all desires known, and from you no secrets are hid:'[1] I bring to you this troubling memory." Take some time to sit alone with the accusation of inadequacy. What percentage of the accusation is true? Own that. But be cautious about taking on too much guilt for a particular incident.

～ Talk out the issue with a spiritual counselor or therapist. Regrets may distract you from other issues lurking below the surface that need to be addressed. It can be too easy to say, "I wasn't the best husband . . ." to elicit support from others. You may be seeking premature absolution.

～ Write out an accusation: "I accuse myself of . . ." and fill in the blank. Then date the indictment. Let it sit. When you revisit it, examine the accusation closely. Is there data to back up the accusation?

Grievers may have unfinished business with a deceased. Some need help in processing the issues. Some grievers are too hard on themselves. Unkindness, regardless of the source, complicates grief. In reality, we sometimes grieve for what we did not do as much as for what we did.

Memories, good and bad,
float into the griever's mind
like menacing rain clouds
over a summer day picnic.

Without excuse or explanation
offer the memory
to Christ.

Some of the unfinished,
committed to His care
will in His good time
be resolved.[2]

Q19 How do I forgive myself?

If after reflection, and perhaps counseling, you conclude you
need to be forgiven for specific acts, pray this wonderful prayer
that has been meaningful to grievers for centuries:

All that we ought to have thought
    and have not thought,
All that we ought to have said,
    and have not said,
All that we ought to have done,
    and have not done;
All that we ought not to have thought,
    and yet have thought,
All that we ought not to have spoken,
    and yet have spoken,
All that we ought not to have done,
    and yet have done;
For thoughts, words and works, pray we,
O God, for forgiveness.[1]

Another suggestion is to write a letter asking for forgiveness. Include every troubling thing. Then consider one of these options:

- Take the letter to the grave or scattering area and read it aloud;
- Take the letter to a place of meaning in your relationship and read it aloud;
- Read the letter to a minister or psychologist.

Then, having read the letter, destroy it.

Eleven words could salvage most regretful relational memories: "*I am sorry. I was wrong. I want to be forgiven.*" Suppose the positions were reversed; you had died, your loved one survived. How would you want your loved one to deal with forgiveness? Ask yourself, "Where is my loved one now? Would she or he be ungracious in forgiving me?"

Q20 I regret not being with my mother when she died. I could not watch her suffer any more. How do I forgive myself?

I was not there when my mother died. I am glad my brother and sister and the in-laws were there when she took her last breath and discovered the promised reality of eternal life. I had been there for four days and nights. Assuming a nurse's assessment to be accurate—that my mother could live another week—I flew home to Kansas City. She died soon after I arrived home.

I spent time thoroughly indicting myself for my decision to fly home. Then someone gave me a gift. After a presentation in which I mentioned my regrets, an individual said, "Have you ever considered the possibility your mother did not want you present when she died? That she had been waiting for you to leave?" I have found comfort in that possibility.

Most of us can convince ourselves that we *could* have, *should* have done more for our loved one. Maybe your mother knew that watching her die was hard on you. It is, after all, rather amazing what mothers know about their children. I am sure she did not think about it twice.

5. Questions about Causation

"In general, however, in our society death is largely
the result of the long-term wearing out of bodily organs,
a deterioration associated with lifestyle, environment,
and aging. That is, people in our society die mainly
of a set of chronic conditions or causes called
degenerative diseases."
—*Charles Corr*[1]

A Comparison of the Ten Leading Causes of Death[2]

1900	*1994*
1. Influenza and pneumonia	Diseases of the heart
2. Tuberculosis	Cancer
3. Gastritis, duodenitis, enteritis	Cerebrovascular diseases
4. Diseases of the heart	Chronic obstructive pulmonary diseases
5. Vascular lesions	Accidents and adverse effects
6. Chronic nephritis (kidneys)	Pneumonia and influenza
7. All accidents	Diabetes mellitus
8. Malignant neoplasms (cancer)	HIV
9. Certain diseases of early infancy	Suicide
10. Diphtheria	Chronic liver disease/cirrhosis

Q21 My friend insists the Bible teaches "all our days are numbered." If it's "our time to go," we die. Is this true?

Adin Steinsaltz, a wise Jewish scholar and rabbi, bemoans the irritating problem of theological "shorthand" thinking.[1] Some grievers seek, sometimes seize, easy answers rather than wrestle with difficult truths. A scripture has to be pondered in light of its historical setting.

Admittedly, two Old Testament verses seemingly support this idea: "Man's days are determined; you have decreed the number of his months and have set times he cannot exceed" (Job 14:5), and "All the days ordained for me were written in your book before one of them came to be" (Psalm 139:16).

Certainly, some individuals believe the length of our lifespan was determined before our first breath, as God "set the timer." In this thinking, you can be in the best medical facility in the country, with the best physicians and the most attentive nursing care, but if your time is up, your time is *up!* Alexandra Mosca observes, "I became convinced that one's date of death is written, metaphorically speaking, in some big book in the sky. Perhaps, it is easier to believe this. The philosophy took away the guilt and 'what ifs' and 'if onlys' individuals felt after someone close had died."[2]

Sometimes, in the laboratory of personal experience, you get to decide what you really believe. As a patient in intensive care in May 1996, I happened to be, at times, unaware of how ill I was. Later, I learned that I could have died because of an irregular heartbeat. In the era before modern medicine, I *would* have died. Yes, some friends told me "it just wasn't your time to go." I choose to believe God was gracious to me.

Life is too mysterious to be so deterministic. I have sat through too many funerals listening to that musical phrase, "His heart is touched by our grief." Although I do not understand why some prayers "work" and some prayers do not, I keep praying. Writing this, I groan out a prayer for a friend who is battling cancer. I keep pleading with God to give her long life because she is such a difference-maker in the world. I am so sad after every visit with her, as it may be my last.

Yes, the psalmist said, "All my days are numbered," but I do not believe that is God's last word on the topic. I have seen too many "walking dead" come back to live a vibrant life, who pulled through and stunned great medical minds. I do not think those individuals lived simply because "it wasn't their time."

Dan Spaite, as a chief of emergency medicine in a medical center in Tucson, has seen lots of individuals "at death's door." He rejects the deterministic school of thought by appealing to the Apostle Paul's words on the near death of his friend, Epaphroditus:[3] "Indeed he was ill, and almost died. But God had mercy on him, and not on him only but also on me, to spare me sorrow upon sorrow" (Philippians 2:27).

Q22 Why is a postmortem examination so important?

Postmortem examinations are a basic component of modern medicine and research. Postmortems:

- Establish the cause of death
- Confirm a clinical diagnosis
- Determine the extent of a disease
- Determine treatment effectiveness
- Determine adverse effects of treatment, diagnostic procedures, or patient-monitoring procedures
- Establish a source of bleeding that may have been undetermined
- Determine the condition of the operative or wound site

Pathologists work diligently to find answers for our "whys." Sometimes, a defect or condition is not known until the postmortem. One study of twenty-five-hundred cases revealed that 40 percent of the autopsies "unearthed a major, unexpected finding that contributed to the death."[1]

While answering questions about the cause of death, autopsy results can also have an impact on blood relatives' health care. For example, some autopsies have verified the existence of Alzheimer's through a postmortem. While that can be a difficult disclosure for the family, it may give some members an awareness needed to plan future medical care.

In a sense, an autopsy is also a family's gift to medical education. Crucial knowledge your physician has today might have been gained from a postmortem following a death that broke another family's heart. Another study of 2,479 autopsies concluded that approximately 10 to 13 percent of postmortems "reveal an unexpected finding that would have changed patient management if the finding had been known prior to the patient's death."[2] For example, individuals died of HIV complications long before the first Centers for Disease Control and Prevention report on AIDS. Only in retrospect, did medical personnel, family, and friends finally understand the cause of death. The value of postmortems can be captured in a paraphrase from a speech by Dr. Martin Luther King Jr., "If I can help somebody as I go along . . . then my [dying] shall not be in vain."

Postmortems are legally essential in cases of murder, suicide, or trauma. We may feel angry with an elderly man driving his car into a school bus, injuring children—until the postmortem demonstrates he had had a heart attack seconds before the collision.

Q23 My husband, age twenty-nine and in great physical shape, just dropped dead. The postmortem was inconclusive. How can I find out why he died?

Between 2 and 4 percent of postmortem examinations are inconclusive, according to Steven Keyser, head of A-Medi-Legal National Autopsy Service.[1] The rate is even higher in cases involving infants: One out of every four perinatal autopsies is inconclusive.[2]

My friend Jay Harrison, a great, caring pathologist who has worked long hours to be able to give families the gift of an explanation, notes that even though a postmortem examination can be inconclusive, it can rule out certain issues. If no trace of cancer is found, some family members will take comfort in that. An inconclusive result can also help the family's attitudes toward physicians, because it shows that nothing was "missed."[3]

Unfortunately, in a hyperlitigious society, some physicians are hesitant to sit down and talk in "lay" terms about a loved one's death. Some specialists see any death of a patient in their care as a failure. Other specialists have poor "people skills"— they are great physicians but you wouldn't want to be stuck on a desert island with them. There is no course in medical school called, "Compassionate Conversation 101."

Some grievers have to learn to live in the absence of a definitive answer.

Do not be intimidated or afraid to talk about the postmortem results with your loved one's doctor. Take some moments to write down your questions. Find a nurse or friend who can help you formulate and rehearse your questions. Make an appointment with the physician or with the pathologist who conducted the examination. Raise your questions and clarify your need for a "better" explanation.

Despite all the scientific advancements, death still remains, in many cases, a mystery. You may be a griever who has to live without an answer, which only makes the absence of your loved one's death more troubling. If your husband's postmortem examination remains inconclusive, and doctors have no more explanations for you, perhaps consider the exam a "gift" to medical research and education.

Q24 Does God inflict death on certain groups of individuals, like people with AIDS?

Unfortunately, there are some people with small hearts who believe certain individuals deserve particular diseases. These people cannot be happy without thinking the entrance ramps to hell are clogged. They want God to be mean-spirited and hardhearted like them. God always says "No!" to this kind of thinking.

God is *not* some Mafia-like bone-breaker who is determined to settle scores. The Jesus-like God I have come to trust doesn't "make nasty." On anyone.

If only we had a bumper sticker that reads, "Viruses happen!" God does not inflict pestilence as punishment. When pestilence—or what we label pestilence—breaks out, God works to stir compassion in the hearts of kind individuals who work hard to make a difference.

You probably have never heard of Hiram Pierce, MD, but I think he's in God's "Hall of Fame." During the Memphis yellow fever epidemic of 1887, when thousands of Memphis residents died and many others fled the city, he left his practice in Cincinnati—even though his father threatened to disown him—and went to Memphis to respond to the call for physicians. Hiram Pierce, age twenty-eight, died in Memphis. But while he lived, he made a difference. Even today, God stirs compassion in the hearts of individuals to do research, to raise money, to bring chicken soup, to lobby legislators for research appropriations, and to file lawsuits—all so other patients receive the care they need.

6. Questions about God

"God is with us at the most terrible moment of our time.
He is not in front to lead, nor behind to push,
not above to protect, but 'Beside us to guide us,
Our God with us joining.'"
—*Peter J. Gomes*[1]

"You should feel free to ask anything and everything
you want to ask. There is so such thing
as a silly theological question, if it's your question."
—*Marianne H. Micks*[2]

Q25 Where was God when my son died?

This common but challenging question is difficult for me to answer. Some friends answer with a tired cliché: "The same place he was when his son died." But that does not provide comfort.

The theologian William Sloane Coffin Jr. certainly experienced angst when his son, Alexander, drowned. Many people expected him to be able to answer the "where was God?" question. They were not prepared for—but found comfort in—his answer:

The one thing that should never be said when someone dies is, 'It is God's will.' Never do we know enough to say that. My own condition lies in knowing that it was not the will of God that [let] Alex die; that when the waves closed over the sinking car, God's heart was the first of all our hearts to break.[1]

In the grief groups I lead, I always ask, "Is anyone in this room angry at God?" Immediately, I get several "Oh no's," but one soft, "I am." In the Bible, Job's wife became infamous for her one-liner, "Curse God and die!" which would have been the easy way out for Job, following the death of his ten children, his animals, and his own physical suffering. I confess that in listening to some grievers' stories, I find myself asking, "God! What were you thinking about on this one?!" I have to ask that to keep my sanity.

Lots of grievers become pragmatic, if temporary, atheists following the death of a loved one. Lots of believers experiencing grief become angry that God is "doing this" to them. Yet in the midst of the darkness, some find strength to forge a new faith, a new perception of God that is not sugarcoated.

Harold Kushner, author of *When Bad Things Happen to Good People,* might well have lived out his life as an anonymous rabbi in Natick, Massachusetts, but for the diagnosis of his three-year-old son, Aaron. Doctors determined the boy had an incurable condition that caused a rapid aging of his body. Aaron died as an adolescent. While Rabbi Kushner had supported others in their journey through grief, now his path was as a principal griever, not a companion. He writes of those early days:

> . . . I was wounded not only by the prospect of losing him but also by the sense that God was doing this to me. Like most of us, I was raised to believe in an all-powerful God who controlled everything that happened in the world, and if we could not understand God's ways, the limitation was ours, not God's.[2]

Kushner had come to believe that because he was a good rabbi and a good man, "partly as a reward, partly as an inducement to those others, God would bless and protect my family." When confronted with the doctors' diagnosis, he explains, "I couldn't help feeling that I had held up my end of the bargain but God had just defaulted on His. It became desperately important for me to know whether God was on my side or on the side of the illness."[3]

In that brutal process of wrestling with his perceptions of God, Kushner determined that principles and forces in the world—be they genetics, laws of nature, fire, or bullets—"harm good people and bad people alike." But, he resolved, "I can handle this because I am not alone. . . . I can handle this because God is with *me* and not on the side of the illness or accident. I can handle this because God is on my side."[4]

Kushner's conclusion echoes the well-known words of the Twenty-third Psalm: "Even though I walk through the valley of the shadow of death, . . . *you are with me*" (verse 4). The theologian Lewis Smedes, whose newborn son died, takes this idea a step further. Years after his son's death, he concluded:

> God was right there doing what God always does in the presence of evil that is willed by humans—resisting it, battling it, trying God's best to keep it from happening. This time evil won. God, we hope will one day emerge triumphant over evil—though, on the way to that glad day, God sometimes takes a beating.[5]

More than once, I have been aboard a plane that has taken off in foggy weather. From the ground, I could not see the sun, but it was there nonetheless. In time, as the plane broke through the fog, we emerged into brilliant sunshine. The experience of grievers such as Kushner and Smedes includes moments of keenly feeling God's absence. But because they chose to trust God for the long haul, they gained a new understanding of God's care. Give God some space in your grief.

Q26 Is it a sin to be angry with God after a loved one's death?

No, but it might be a sin to pretend you are not angry. God knows all already. Robert Schuller once told Larry King, "Nothing is more important than honesty in prayer. There are no pretensions in prayer, so the best place is wherever you are."[1] Acknowledge your anger and your powerlessness. I like John Hewett's words, "God is the only one prepared to handle all your anger at him. If you are ticked off at the Almighty, for his sake (and yours) tell him!"[2]

I appreciate individuals who do not camouflage feelings. Christian entertainer Sheila Walsh said following the death of a friend's child, "If You took my son, I wouldn't doubt that You were alive; I just wouldn't talk with You anymore."[3]

Let your anger rip for the sake of others in your life. Otherwise, you will direct your anger at them.

Q27 My mother repeatedly says, "I don't understand why God took your father." Does God go around with a list of those he is "taking" today?

This question has a hint of one of those not-yet-successfully-resolved questions that has plagued grievers since death one. Job, following the death of his ten children and masses of animals, said, "The Lord gave and the Lord has taken away; may the name of the Lord be praised" (Job 1:21). At age ten I heard this verse given as an explanation for the death of my minister's three-year-old. Some individuals, when in doubt, quote—or unleash—Scripture, unaware that Scriptures can bruise as readily as ill-chosen words.

Some people are determined to defend the sovereignty of God. Nothing happens—not even a bird falls—without the Lord's approval. Some will not, of course, put God's fingerprints on a death. Rather, they hedge, "God allowed this." Or it was

"God's will." That was the position of former Surgeon General C. Everett Koop when his son, David, died in a mountain climbing accident. "God was able, but in His sovereignty, He chose not to" prevent the death.[1] Not everyone can live with such a conclusion or be comfortable around individuals who come to such a conclusion.

Victor Parachin reminds grievers, "Rather than talking about God's 'taking' a love one, it is more theologically accurate to place the focus on God's 'receiving and welcoming' a loved one."[2] I too believe God opens his arms wide to receive his children. I prefer the King James rendition of Jesus's promise of eternal life. "I go to prepare a place for you. And if I go and prepare a place for you, I will come again, and receive you unto myself; that where I am, there ye may be also" (John 14:2-3).

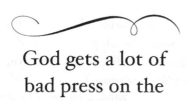

God gets a lot of bad press on the sovereignty issue.

Years ago Christians found great meaning in singing at funerals, "Safe in the arms of Jesus," particularly when death was a result of violence. We sometimes even desire our loved ones to go to Jesus to escape pain. I once knelt on the floor beside my mother's bed and pleaded with God to "take her" and end the suffering she and her children and grandchildren were experiencing. God did not "take" my mother in my time framework.

I have been moved on several occasions by the Swedish hymn, "Children of the Heavenly Father" particularly the lyrics, "Though he giveth or he taketh, God his children ne'er forsaketh; His the loving purpose solely, To preserve them pure and holy."[3]

God allows more human freedom than I would if I were God. Thus, Lee Harvey Oswald had the freedom that day in November 1963 to take a rifle and blow away the life of a husband and father of two small children who just happened to be the president of the United States. In that moment, why didn't God "take"—if he was going to meet a quota of "takens" that day—Lee Harvey Oswald?

Robert Dallek's title for his biography *An Unfinished Life: John F. Kennedy, 1917-1963* could apply to many individuals. It is sometimes not so much the cause of death that troubles us but the unfinishedness of a life, or relationships, or futures. Someone has said it's not the dates on the tombstone that count but the dash between the dates. What did the person do—and what are we doing—with the dash?

Q28 Does anyone have "a right to die"?

Historically, it has been understood that an individual does not have a right to die, or as some would phrase it, "to play God." It was understood that individuals were part of a community; thus, the individual's life and death had an impact on the whole community.

Christians have pondered Paul's guidance, "You are not your own; you were bought at a price." The next phrase, traditionally applied to sexual choices, has implications in this arena as well. "Therefore honor God with your body" (1 Corinthians 6:19-20). Ethicist Gilbert Meilaender comments:

> [Christians] do not approach this issue by thinking in terms of a "right to life" or a "right to die with dignity." That is to say, we do not start with the language of independence. Within the story of my life I have the relative freedom of a creature, but it is not simply "my" life to do with as I please. I am free to end it, of course, but not free to do so without risking something as important to my nature as freedom: namely, the sense of myself as one who always exists in relation to God.[1]

The devout individualism so highly prized in contemporary society has turned "rights" into a hot issue. One factor fueling

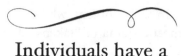

Individuals have a right to die in the absence of pain.

the debate on "right to die" is the scandalous lack of pain management for the terminally ill. Diane Meier, MD, reports that oncologists believe two-thirds of their patients suffer significant pain. She also relates that in a study of nine thousand hospitalized dying patients, half of them "experienced moderate to severe pain during their last seventy-two hours of life."[2] Why? It is excruciating for individuals to watch a loved one die in pain. At one point, as my mother died, my sister turned to me and said in tears, "I wouldn't let a dog die this way!"

Kenneth Vaux and Sara Vaux have created a conceptualization of "a good death." A good death is ending one's days:

- Relieved of disabling pain
- Surrounded by family and friends
- Attended by sensitive caregivers
- Reconciled with all persons
- In justice and humanity with the world
- At peace with God[3]

A "good death" means that we do not die alone. The Bible uses a wonderful phrase, "gathered to his people" (Genesis 35:29) to describe dying. In *Finding Your Way to Say Goodbye*, I wrote, "Part of a good death is gathering those individuals we have loved to be 'with us' before and as we set off for our ultimate bon voyage."[4]

Q29   Do babies become angels?

Some well-meaning individuals have attempted to defang the death of a child by suggesting the child is now an angel, "up there looking out for me, for us." The phrase "my/our little angel" has been carved on thousands of gravestones. For some grieved parents, initially, that may be comforting.

From a Christian perspective, however, although the image is sentimental, for a baby to become an angel would be a stepping down from their status as a human being, a child of God.

Q30 How does God respond to individuals who die who are not Christians?

Historically, two destinations, heaven and hell, have dominated Protestant thinking. Grace is demonstrated in Jesus's encounter with the thief on the cross who whispered, "Jesus, remember me when you come into your kingdom." Jesus responded, with no hesitation, "I tell you the truth, today you will be with me in paradise" (Luke 23:43).

Traditional Christian faith has always pointed to Jesus's words, "I am the way and the truth and the life. No one comes to the Father except through me" (John 14:6), interpreting the words to mean "Nothing personal, but no non-Christians allowed." Increasingly, in a pluralistic society, inclusiveness is troublesome and is being challenged—not always in public discussion but in private reflection. Over the years, some Christians have accepted a doctrine called universalism as an answer for this dilemma. Universalists believe God will work to bring all humans into relationship and eternal life with him. Some universalists cite John 3:17, "For God did not send his Son into the world to condemn the world."

Kenneth Kantzer, former editor of *Christianity Today*, acknowledges the discomfort of many Christians. "How can I be happy in heaven if I know some dark corner of the universe contains human beings who are consciously suffering eternal torment? For that matter, how can I be happy in heaven if I know God has erased from existence—annihilated—my own dearly beloved son or daughter. My emotions shout, 'No, it cannot be.'"[1] Nevertheless, Kantzer notes that twelve times in the New Testament Jesus himself mentioned hell. "Then he will say to those on his left, 'Depart from me, you who are cursed, into the eternal fire prepared for the devil and his angels'" (Matthew 25:41) and "Then they will go away to eternal punishment, but the righteous to eternal life" (verse 46).

Fundamentalist and evangelical Christians believe all individuals who have not been "born again" or in their phrasing, "who have not accepted Jesus *as their personal Lord and Savior*" will go to hell. Anne Graham Lotz, daughter of Billy Graham, voices the perspective of many conservative evangelical Christians when she sidesteps the notion that God sends anyone to hell:

> God is not arbitrary or whimsical. He extends to all His generous invitation to claim His House as our eternal home. If we accept His invitation, we live with Him forever. However, if we do not accept because we refuse His only Son as our Savior, then we exclude ourselves from My Father's House. It's our choice.[2]

In responding to this question, some turn to Paul's list in 1 Corinthians, "Do you not know that the wicked will not inherit the kingdom of God? Do not be deceived: Neither the sexually immoral nor idolaters nor adulterers nor male prostitutes nor homosexual offenders nor thieves nor the greedy nor drunkards nor slanderers nor swindlers will inherit the kingdom of God" (verses 9-10). Unfortunately, out of Paul's list of those who will not be "invited," the focus tends, these days, to fall on people who are homosexual, which is rather amazing given the epidemic preponderance of greed, adultery, idolatry, and lying.

We would do well to ponder the possibility that God is more outrageously gracious than our expectations.

Some evangelical Christians tend to be a wee bit selective in reprioritizing Paul's list. Pat Robertson, for example, insists that Paul "pulls no punches" on hell's demographics. "Those who have engaged in homosexual behavior will not enter the kingdom of heaven, unless they are cleansed by the blood of Christ. Those who continue a homosexual lifestyle after receiving knowledge of the truth run a similar risk."[3]

Although hell is a hard sell in this "live and let live" culture, *USA Today* reports that 71 percent of Americans believe in hell, up from 56 percent in 1997.[4] We would do well to ponder the possibly that God is more outrageously gracious than our expectations.

Q31 How do I convince a friend that God did not cause her child's death?

You will not convince your friend. You can be God's ambassador of caring to your friend. You can listen to questions, allegations, and ramblings. You can "be present to" that individual. Paul insisted that while God "comforts us in all our troubles" he does it *"so that* we can comfort those in any trouble with the comfort we ourselves have received from God" (2 Corinthians 1:4).

Peter J. Gomes, who has listened to many grieving students, alumni, faculty, and staff as minister of Harvard University's Memorial Chapel, reminds grievers, "God is to be found where God is most needed—in trouble, sorrow, sickness, adversity, and even death itself."[1]

7. Questions about Grief and Spirituality

"Our ancestors had to deal with the losses of life,
but they did not turn to therapy. Instead the generations
before us looked to the oldest reservoirs of human
wisdom—religious traditions."
—*David Wolpe*[1]

"A great religious tradition has
its own vocabulary and insight."
—*David Wolpe*[2]

"For me, spirituality is a quest for meaning
and an opportunity to make one's life important.
This is my one shot to be who I am and I'd better do it!"
—*Jack Morgan*[3]

Q32 I miss my spouse the most at church. I just
cannot concentrate. We attended the same
church for forty-six years and raised our
children in this church. Is this unusual?

No, it is not unusual. Remember the lyrics to the song, "I'll Be Seeing You"? One of the tasks of grief is to deal with the absence in familiar places and spaces. William Worden insisted the third major task of grief is: "To adjust to environments in which the person . . . is missing."[1] If you have attended a church for forty-six years you probably "miss" him lots of places in that sacred space—in the foyer, in the sanctuary, at the communion rail, in the fellowship hall, in a classroom, even in the parking lot. Indeed, some individuals try to talk grievers out of having funerals or memorial services in sacred places. "Every time you look toward the front, you will see that casket or urn!"

Some individuals, in a sense, had a chance to "try out" their spouses' absence by attending church and going places alone during periods in which their spouses were ill or could not go out. For those experiencing a sudden death, the absence is immediate and intense.

You may want to take your time returning to your community of faith. I know this sounds heretical but you can face a *tsunami* of grief the first Sundays you attend after a death when the absence of presence is keenly felt. It may start with a simple thing like having to park your car (before your husband let you out and he parked the car.) Many congregants have "their" places to sit in a congregation. Now that space feels odd, irregular. One woman told me she always went two spaces into the pew because her husband loved to talk in the foyer and would eventually join her. She asked, "How do I break that habit?"

When you're ready, you may choose to attend a later or earlier service. Or sit in a different place. Some churches offer different styles of worship: contemporary or traditional. You may want to attend a different service, which will mean you meet new individuals who did not know you as part of a couple.

Breathe a prayer before you enter the church. "Lord, help me do this." Remember those friends who promised, "Let me know if there is anything I can do . . ." Ask them to sit with you or if you can sit with them.

Grace can be found when we acknowledge our grief in those places of sacred meaning and memory in our lives.

Consider taking a sabbatical from your community of faith. Some individuals find the memories in a particular community of faith initially overwhelming. Attend some different congregations. This may feel like betraying the support you have received from a congregation, but most friends will understand.

Peggy and Bob Benson were pillars in a congregation for years. Then, as a widow, Peggy felt the need to "migrate" to a new community of faith. While those parishioners "sat up and cried with me, prayed with me . . . took me into their homes when I didn't much want to go back to my empty one, they helped me pack up furniture and get through the holidays and took me out to dinner when I was lonely . . ." they also reminded her of a past, a past with Bob, a past as a couple. She continues:

> I was sitting in a Sunday morning service there one day, when I realized that I couldn't be there among them anymore. I looked around at the familiar faces. Faces I had known for a long time. . . .
>
> But I also had come to see that the faces that I loved and the familiar surroundings and traditions and movements were somehow working together to keep me from worshiping. While the congregation was gathering each Sunday 'in remembrance of Him,' I was gathering up to remember that which was lost.[2]

The migration, she found, can be a tough adjustment "between a place too familiar for me to be able to worship just now and a place too new for me to be able to find community just yet." But the process can teach us about ourselves.

Whether or not you change churches, expect some "down the road" spiritual ambushes. It could be on All Saint's Day, Mother's or Father's Day, or during Advent or Christmas, particularly the first one, that you feel ambushed by a fresh awareness of your loss. Caroline Kennedy once explained, "You don't think about it all the time. Sometimes you're just walking down the street and it just hits you, you know. It just hits you."[3]

Talk to your minister about your grief experience. You may be able to broaden her or his understanding of bereavement. Admittedly, the minister may know something about grief in general but not about your particular grief. What she learns from you will help another griever on another day.

Q33 I do not know how I would have made it through this without my church family. I miss, however, being included in couples' social events. How can I avoid feeling "left out?"

Grieving individuals are subject to "left out" feelings. In reality, some friends, afraid of our grief, do not invite us to certain social events unless we promise to "behave." (That request is understood rather than stated.) No breaking down, no crying, no sadness to spoil the festive mood for everyone else. An empty place at what was once a table for four can be threatening and predictive. Oftentimes, invitations to couples' outings become invitations for just the wives (or just the husbands) to go to lunch.

Your presence at a church meal function may be unnerving. Ever notice how we tend to eat in "even" numbers in church settings? I can count on one hand the number of church meals in which the place settings have been in odd numbers. Remember it is not you; it is your circumstances that alter the social invitations even within the life of a community of faith.

Q34 I cannot pray. I hear some talk about what a strength prayer is. What if prayer does not do anything for me?

Vance Havner counseled, "Pray as you can—not as you can't."[1] Some of the most elegant prayers prayed by grievers are two-worded, "Oh God . . ." Grievers often use lots of exclamation marks or question marks in prayers.

Some grievers sit in silence with God. Mother Teresa once advised a person seeking guidance on prayer technique that "it is in the silence of the heart God speaks. God is the friend of silence—we need to listen to God because it is not what we say but what He says to us that matters."[2]

Sometimes we have too narrow a definition of prayer. Some of the things we may not label as prayer are, in fact, from God's perspective, prayerful. Donna Schaper, who has counseled many on a grief trail, believes sighs can be prayer too.[3]

Some grievers discover that prayer can be creative. I heard a story about a widower who sat for hours in a Catholic church. One day the priest said, "I notice you here a lot. I admire your prayer life."

"Oh, I am not praying," he replied. "I come here to tell jokes to God."

Three centuries ago Paul Gerhardt, in a hymn text, urged grievers in his congregation:

"Commit thou all thy griefs
    And ways into his hands.
God hears thy sighs and counts thy tears;
    God shall lift up thy head."[4]

Many grievers have "borrowed" a prayer when they were too grieved or too angry to be creative or imaginative. Try the Lord's Prayer, the Twenty-Third Psalm, or any of the "lament" psalms (especially 3, 5, 6, 7, 13). The Psalms have been the lament-soaked prayer book of millions of grievers.

Some grievers have found the hymnal a prayer resource when they cannot pray. Pray Isaac Watts' hymn text:

"O God, our help in ages past,
Our hope for years to come,
Our shelter from the stormy blast,
And our eternal home."[5]

Across the years, countless grievers have found this hymn a source of strength. Leo Rosten reminds grievers, "A place in Heaven is reserved for those who weep but cannot pray."[6]

Q35 Why should I pray? God did not answer my prayers for my husband to live! I prayed and prayed and prayed. I do not want to hear, "God answers prayer!"

Prayer is not deal making. Sometimes God does seem in absentia in our lives. I experienced that absence as I sat through the night watching my mother die. How many times did I plead, "God, take her and end the suffering," knowing I meant my suffering as well as hers?

Sometimes we do not feel like praying. Ed Dobson is learning a great deal about prayer as he battles Lou Gehrig's Disease. After a lifetime of preaching, teaching, and writing about prayer, he says, "My natural assumption was that this suffering would lift my prayer life to levels it has never known before. The truth was, I didn't feel like praying. I didn't feel like talking to God."[1]

Stephen Broyles had a chance to learn a lot about prayer during the illness of and following the death of his wife that left him a single parent. Like so many other faith-oriented grievers, he looked for insight in the experience of Job, the "patron saint of grievers."[2] It's easy to focus on the boils of Job and overlook the ten griefs of Job; his seven sons and three daughters died.

Job's net worth evaporated in a matter of hours. Yet, he said, "Though he slay me, yet will I hope in him" (Job 13:15).

Untold thousands of Christians prayed for Gracia and Martin Burnham, missionaries in the Philippines, while the Abu Sayyaf rebels held them captive for a year. In a shootout between the rebels and the Filipino army attempting to rescue them, Martin was killed. In her book, *In the Presence of My Enemies*, Gracia acknowledges that she cannot explain why so many prayers for the safe rescue of both were not granted.[3]

It is tough, for some, when others get their miracles. Your loved one's hospital roommate got well or got the transplant. Why didn't God see fit to give you the miracle he gave to someone else down the hall or with whom you shared a waiting room?

Some grievers pray their way into a new understanding of the loss. Some take a prayer sabbatical. God can handle our silences and our anger.

Even Jesus did not have a 100 percent return on his prayers. In the garden he prayed, "may this cup be taken from me." (And he did not timidly pray.) But the cup had Jesus's name on it.

Grievers learn, often painfully, that God is not predictable. Prayer is not a charm to coerce God into our point of view.

Maybe you think Jesus had it all figured out that night in his darkness. Did Jesus know he would have to die? Then why did he even bother to pray, "My Father, *if it is possible*, may this cup be taken from me" (Matthew 26:39). If anyone should have gotten a prayer answered, it was Jesus.

What I have learned is this: God comes to us in our angry grief, our "I cannot believe it!" grief. He shows up long before we invite him or before we recognize his presence. God can definitely handle our angry, zinger prayers.

Sue Anderson Jenkins' first husband's plane was shot down over Laos back in January 1968. For months she didn't know his fate. "For some time," she recalls, "I didn't know whether I was married or a widow. One evening, God said: 'I have him right here with me. You don't have to pray for him as a prisoner anymore.'"[4]

In 2003, Jenkins was notified that her first husband's remains and his wedding band had been, at last, found at the scene of the crash. She considered that ring proof of his death and a gift from God.

God does not "take away" our grief; rather he shows up in our grief. God never abandons any one in grief. He gives us courage to confront our grief, and he will work in our grief to make us wiser, stronger, and more caring. I am moved at funerals whenever I hear these words in a song, "Be not afraid, I go before you, come follow me and I will give you rest."[5] With that rest comes confidence.

Q36 My mother died a painful death. I am tired of hearing, "You should be grateful you had your mother so long." What do I have to be grateful for?

Gratitude is an essential element in the integration of a grief into our lives. If you focus on only your suffering, you heighten your anxiety.

Remember, not everyone had a "loved one." For some individuals, the deceased is the "unloved one" or "once-loved one."

Spend some time formulating a list of ten things you have to be grateful for. For example, you may be grateful your mother had good nursing care. You may be grateful you lived near your mother and could spend time with her. You could be grateful for the sacrifices your mother made for you. You could be grateful for the support of your supervisor at work.

Next, rehearse those gratitudes aloud. Tell them to a complete stranger. Carry the list with you. Add new gratitudes to the list.

Pray your gratitudes:

"God, I am grateful for all the sacrifices my mother made for me."

"God, I am grateful for my mother's faith that she passed on to me."

"God, I am grateful for my mother's unshakeable belief in me."

"God, I am grateful for . . ."

Yes, there may be things for which you are not grateful. Be grateful for even small things. Concentrate on your gratitudes and you will experience a different aspect of grief. You may want to pray, "God, in time, would you help me to be grateful for . . ."

Finally, some individuals have found it helpful to pray through a prayer book such as *Prayers for Those Who Mourn, Life Prayers from Around the World,* or *The Little Book of Prayers* (see Appendix B for a list of prayer resources for grievers). Borrowing another's words of prayer will help you jump-start your words.

Sometimes, a major element of prayer is simply showing up. The ancient Hebrews asked, "How can we sing the songs of the Lord while in a foreign land?" (Psalm 137:1). Grief is definitely a strange land. Start your mornings with this question, "Lord, how shall I sing your song today in a foreign land called grief?" End your day with gratitude, "Lord, thank you for being with me this day in this strange land called grief."

8. Questions about Forgiveness

> "There may be some issues that need to be examined, and
> you may need to work through the process of receiving
> forgiveness from God and from yourself. Most of us,
> however, simply need to stop whipping ourselves
> and start comforting ourselves."
> —*Dick Gilbert*[1]

Q37 How do I forgive the man who killed my father?

Some grievers would answer, "You just forgive them." However, whether your father's death happened intentionally or accidentally, whether the person who caused the death feels remorse or not, forgiveness will probably not be easy for you. And if the death happened when you were a child, the death not only robbed you of a parent but also the innocence of childhood.

I worry about premature forgiveness, a forgiveness granted begrudgingly because the victim feels helpless or powerless. Real forgiveness is rarely instantaneous. Usually over time, you realize feelings of "unforgivingness" no longer take up as much space as it once did.

Sometimes forgiveness is proportional. "God, I just cannot forgive this individual. But I am willing to forgive 10 percent. As you help me with that 10 percent, I will give you another 10 percent. Then, with your grace, finally I can forgive the entire thing."

Q38 How do I forgive the driver of the car that struck and killed my child?

Accidents do happen. Sometimes they happen because drivers are young or immature; other times drivers allowed themselves to be distracted for a moment. Each year, more than seventeen thousand U.S. citizens die in alcohol-related automobile incidents; another 500,000 are injured.[1] MADD, or Mothers Against Drunk Drivers, contends that when individuals who have been drinking get behind the wheel of an automobile, any resulting crash is no accident.

I have heard stories of the victim's loved ones immediately saying, "I forgive you." The sentiment here is similar to Jesus's words from Luke 23:34, "Forgive them, because they do not know what they are doing." Yet, I strongly caution you, do not grant premature absolution. The rush to forgiveness often results in cheap forgiveness or sloppy, sentimental, "it is what Jesus would do" forgiveness. Fast-track forgiveness prevents us from doing the spiritual exercises of examining our attitudes toward the driver.

I think a wrestled forgiveness has the best potential of lasting. One griever I met "forgave" the driver who did not see his daughter and struck and killed her. But he worked at his grief, reading every library book on the topic he could find. And he worked to see that a traffic signal was installed in that space so another father would not have to "forgive" a driver following an accident in that location.

I know Jesus asked the Father to forgive the persons who crucified him. I am not Jesus. I will need time to forgive those who have forever altered my relational narrative.

On the other hand, what happens if I do not forgive this individual? Anyone can be angry or stay angry following a death, but they risk poisoning other relationships. A group of individuals chose to found Mothers Against Drunk Drivers to do something "with" their anger. Through the work of this organization, alcohol-related incidents have declined 43 percent.[2] It is what you do *with* your anger that can make a difference.

Q39 How do I forgive God for taking my only child?

You begin by admitting you do not want to forgive him. Some would say, begrudgingly, "I have to forgive him. He's God." Others would challenge any notion of God needing to be forgiven.

Lewis Smedes, a minister and ethicist, had to face his own personalized Golgotha when his son died "before he had lived the whole of a day."[1] Lewis and his wife had struggled with infertility, so the birth of the child was a cause for celebration. But it quickly turned into a nightmare. Smedes, as a heart-broken father, had to reexamine what he had long believed and the guidance he had given other grievers:

> Because of my Calvinism, God's face had had the unmovable serenity of an absolute sovereign absolutely in control of absolutely everything. Every good thing, every bad thing, every triumph, every tragedy, from the fall of every sparrow to the ascent of every rocket, everything was under God's silent, strange and secretive control.[2]

That unshakable certainly—in the face of other individual's tragedies—had worked for Smedes until those first moments of personal grief, tasting the salt of his own tears, and experiencing the wracked sorrow of his wife. "God's face has never looked the same to me since."[3]

Lots of grievers can identify with Smedes' statement. In grief, this ethicist faced a fork in the spiritual road. He could not believe that God, who had blessed them with an unlikely conception, would turn around and "take" the boy. "I could not believe that God was in control of our child's dying."[4] Had Smedes clung to certitude, he would have missed countless opportunities to care for other parents in grief. He explains:

> I could never again believe that God had arranged for our tiny child to die before he had hardly begun to live, any more than I could believe that we would, one fine day when he would make it all plain, praise God that it had happened.[5]

Smedes added, "with one morning's wrenching intuition, I knew that my portrait of God would have to be repainted."[6] Through your wrestling with your questions you may have to repaint your portrait of God.

Q40 How can I forgive God for allowing my spouse to die? We had just retired and were going to travel and enjoy each other and the grandchildren.

The "golden" years do not happen for everyone, as your question indicates. Harold Kushner attracted a great deal of attention and readers with the title of his best-seller, *When Bad Things Happen to Good People*. Bad things *do* happen to good individuals who have worked hard so they might enjoy their retirement together.

You did not indicate the cause of your husband's death. In some cases, retirement prompts a crisis for type A personalities who have long defined themselves by their jobs or positions or roles. Without employment, they ask, "Who am I now?" Other individuals reap the consequences of high-stress work styles and do not get to enjoy the retirement for which they have worked so hard.

Peter Gomes comments that when bad things happen, "we feel that something has gone terribly wrong. God is not supposed to behave that way. That's not part of the deal." Gomes goes on to say, "God is with us at the most terrible moment" of our lives. "He is not in front to lead, not behind to push, not above to protect," but in the words of the hymn text, "Beside us to guide us, Our God with us joining."[1]

Spend some time reading through the Psalms. Start with 22:1: "My God, my God, why have you forsaken me? Why are you so far from saving me, so far from the words of my groaning?" Grievers for three thousand years, in more languages than can be counted, have recited this and similar themed psalms.

Sometimes, you must pray: "God, help me to forgive you." Sometimes, you must live your way into forgiving God.

Ask your minister, priest, a skilled pastoral counselor, hospital chaplain, or hospice staff to help you find a "griever-friendly" therapist. Unfortunately, not all therapists support thorough grief—a few even take pride in their ability to get counselees "over" their grief. Compassionate therapists walk with you *into* the issues—issues of which you may be unaware but that may be fueling feelings of unforgivingness.

I applaud you for voicing the question. Lots of grievers are "mad as hell" at God but will not admit it. He already knows!

Q41 How do I live with the fact that the person who murdered my son got off on a technicality?

After the murder of a family member or friend, many individuals feel victimized twice: once by the murderer and the other by the criminal justice system. Some grievers fiercely argue that "criminal justice" is an oxymoron in their experience. A procedural issue may provide the loophole that sets the accused free. A conviction in a lower court may be reversed on appeal. The trial process may drag out for years when the victim's loved ones just want "to move on."

Grievers rightfully have difficulty living with the reality when their loved one is dead and the killer, or the accused killer, is "walking free." But some grievers do not want justice—they want vengeance. They want "an eye for an eye, a tooth for a tooth." Ironically, you can get the eye or tooth of presumed justice and still not have peace.

The criminal justice system cannot give you back your loved one's life. Nor can it give you back the energy you have expended seeking your definition of justice. Some grievers find hope in a sense of ultimate, "some day" justice coming from God. Just as one "commits" the body of the dead to the earth, sometimes one must "commit" the claim checks for justice to God's timing. Some individuals have pursued radical justice, choosing to "forgive" the murderer and possibly even create some type of relationship with him or her. Not everyone, I would concede, can do that.

Q42 How do I forgive friends who promised to support me but have not been there for me since my loss?

One widow told me, "After a death you find out who your friends—your *real* friends—are!" We need to realize some individuals make promises at a funeral or memorial service because they are uncomfortable with you, with death, or with being in a funeral home. So the promise of support is little more than an easy cliché: "You just call me if there is anything I can do." Thomas Merton contended that some well-meaning individuals "secrete clichés."[1]

Joseph Scriven raised the point in "What a Friend We Have in Jesus": "Do thy friends despise, forsake thee?" Then he offered sage advice, "Take it to the Lord in prayer." He learned this first-hand by experiencing unsupportive friends following the deaths of two fiancées.[2]

Sometimes, we have to audit our resentment. Did we follow-up on the offer? Did we ask specifically or generically? In today's busy world, individuals have to be reminded of promises of support. Blessed are those whose support brigade works like clockwork.

9. Questions about Eternal Life, Heaven, and Hell

"For hope in eternal life is not some unverifiable curiosity
tacked on as an appendage to faith but is faith in the living,
creating God carried to its radical depths. It is faith in God
that does not stop halfway but follows the road consistently
to the end, trusting that the One who calls things from
nothingness into being, can, and in fidelity does,
call them also from death to new life."
—*Elizabeth A. Johnson*[1]

Q43 Isn't heaven a fairy tale, a spin on "and they
all lived happily ever after"? Can anyone
prove there is a heaven?

Heaven is not a fairy tale. Adherents of all three major
monotheistic religions—Islam, Judaism, and Christianity—
believe in heaven. Christians believe heaven is a gift of a gracious God. The longing for heaven (what I call "the real
country") is placed within our spiritual DNA. The writer of
Ecclesiastes wrote that God has "set eternity in the hearts of

men" (3:11). Jesus comforted his disciples with these words now cherished by the dying and the grieving:

> Do not let your hearts be troubled. Trust in God; trust also in me. In my Father's house are many rooms; if it were not so, I would have told you. I am going there to prepare a place for you. And if I go and prepare a place for you, I will come back and take you to be with me that you may be where I am (John 14:1-3).

In the book of Revelation, the writer, John, describes his vision of a new heaven and a new earth:

> And I heard a loud voice from the throne saying, "Now the dwelling of God is with men, and he will live with them. They will be his people, and God himself will be with them and be their God. He will wipe every tear from their eyes. There will be no more death or mourning or crying or pain, for the old order of things has passed away" (Revelation 21:3-4).

Admittedly, some who believe in heaven have gotten a little carried away in speculating on heaven's topography. Heaven is more about presence than landscape. Jesus's promise is clear: "I go to prepare a place for you." Because Jesus was raised from the dead, we believe we will be raised, too. "Christ has indeed been raised from the dead, the first fruits of those who have fallen asleep. . . . For as in Adam all die, so in Christ all will be made alive" (1 Corinthians 15:20, 22).

I appreciate these words about heaven:

> I really don't think of Heaven so much as a place of rest and golden streets, as I think of it as a place where I can serve God unshackled from my present limitations of finiteness, which so often get in the way when I'm trying to serve His creation.[1]

While I do not comprehend all the details of heaven, nevertheless, I am confident it is going to be good. C. S. Lewis, well acquainted with grief, observed:

> A continual looking forward to the eternal world is not a form of escapism or wishful thinking, but one of the things a Christian is meant to do. It does not mean that we are to leave the present world as it is. If you read history, you will find that the Christians who did the most for the present world were just those who thought most of the next.[2]

Q44 My grandson wants to know when his sister is coming home. How do I explain the permanence of death to a four-year-old?

A child's maturity level influences his or her ability to understand the permanence of death. Remember, today's explanation does not have to be the final answer.

Sometimes family members or friends share an explanation that seems, at the time, reasonable but becomes problematic. For example, soon after the death of President John F. Kennedy, Maude Shaw, the White House nanny, explained his absence to six-year-old Caroline "He's gone to look after Patrick [the Kennedy's two-day-old son who had died]. Patrick was so lonely in heaven. He didn't know anyone there. Now he has the best friend anyone could have. And your father will be very glad to see Patrick."[1] Young John asked, "Did Daddy take his big plane with him?" When Miss Shaw answered yes, John responded, "I wonder when he's coming back."[2]

You might try: "Remember when we were playing at the park and you didn't want to come home? Well, heaven is such a wonderful place that no one ever wants to come home."

Others would counsel a straightforward approach: "When individuals go to heaven they cannot come back to earth."

Q45 I think you get heaven in this life. If one has lived a good life, why does she need an afterlife?

For many people, there is too much hell in this life for this to be heaven. Admittedly, a lot of individuals have difficulty believing in an afterlife, especially in a heaven depicted as "pie-in-the-sky-in-the-by-and-by." We quip, "You only go around once," or "Grab all the gusto you can while you can." Millions of individuals live by a philosophy of "eat, drink, and be merry" for tomorrow you will be dead. Others believe this life is a preparation for the life to come, something of an apprenticeship.

Not everyone gets the "good life." Some individuals know ramifications of injustice that I hope never to know. Many have longingly sang, "There's a better home a-waiting in the sky, Lord, in the sky." Maybe that is too sentimental for you but some find great hope in singing their longings.

C. S. Lewis said no event shaped his belief in heaven as much as the unexpected death of his friend Charles Williams; up to that time, heaven had been a subject of fascination and wonderment. Now heaven became a longed-for reality. Their friendship had been too short. He explains:

> No event has so corroborated my faith in the next world as Williams did simply by dying. When the idea of death and the idea of Williams thus met in my mind, it was the idea of death that was changed.[1]

I do not understand heaven. I do, however, confidently trust the One who promises that heaven ultimately means "to be" with him beyond the dimensional realities of my current body and mind. Otherwise, I have to focus my life on what I can do to be remembered or to leave my mark on this world. Stephen Broyles writes of the limited alternative to eternal life,

Be happy to live a good, solid life on a human scale. Do good work. Enjoy the pleasures of family and friends. . . . Carve out your small and temporary space in the larger human story, knowing that the story will continue after you and will be affected—even if only in a modest degree—by you having been here and by your being remembered by the few who knew you."[2]

As I understand it, as good as that can be, Jesus offers a better and bigger invitation: to be part of an *eternal* story. He will remember me, regardless of how poorly or inadequately or fearfully I have lived. I find great comfort in the dying thief's request, "Jesus, remember me when you come into your kingdom" (Luke 23:42), and Jesus's passionate immediate response, "Today you will be with me in paradise" (verse 43).

Q46 Who gets into heaven?

John Newton, who wrote the lyrics for "Amazing Grace," reportedly expected to find three surprises in heaven: first, that he is there; second, who is not there that he assumed would be there; and third, who is there that he never dreamed would be there. I suspect there will be a pouting section for new arrivals who cannot believe so-and-so is there after what they did. That's when Jesus will laugh, "Yeah, grace is outrageously amazing, isn't it?"

Jesus said, "I am the way and the truth and the life. No one comes to the Father except through me" (John 14:6). In this era of tolerance and diversity, this

I am not the gatekeeper. Heaven is God's party, and God makes up the guest list!

verse troubles some. Poet Maya Angelou questions where her loved ones go, asking, "Are they, as the poet James Weldon Johnson said, 'resting in the bosom of Jesus'? If so, what about my Jewish loves, my Japanese dears, and my Muslim darlings? Into whose bosom are they cuddled?"[1]

Once I could have given a clear-cut answer. I saw the world in rigid terms, the includeds and excludeds. A black spiritual says, "Everybody talkin' about heaven ain't going there." As I have aged, increasingly have I come to cherish the promise of the hymn, "There's a wideness in God's mercy, like the wideness of the sea."[2]

Q47 What do I tell someone who lost a loved one who was not a Christian? How can I give them hope?

This is a tough question. The Roman Catholic Mass contains a phrase about those whose faith is known "only to God." I have long relied on a rather obscure verse in the Old Testament, "Like water spilled on the ground, which cannot be recovered, so we must die. But God does not take away life; instead, he devises ways so that a banished person may not remain estranged from him" (2 Samuel 14:14).

I do not comprehend God's grace. As I understand scripture, God seeks, initiates, pursues. Will God take anyone's "no" for a final answer? Is "whoever" in John 3:16 *whoever*? God is far more gracious and outrageous in defining "whoever" than I am. I also find great hope in Jesus's words, "I say to you that many will come from the east and the west, and will take their places at the feast with Abraham, Isaac, and Jacob in the kingdom of heaven" (Matthew 8:11).

Certainly, others feel differently. For them, the only question is, "Was the deceased saved?" Albert Hsu writes out of a conservative evangelical framework after his father committed suicide: "We simply do not know the ultimate fate of those who are gone. But God gives us hope. Not certainty, but hope."[1] Hsu continues:

It is not for us to speculate on a suicide's final destination. I have stopped worrying about my father's eternal fate. It does me no good to wonder about things that are impossible to know. . . . While I am hopeful that I will see my father again someday, I cannot cling to a false hope and claim with certainty that he is in heaven. That is not for me to say.[2]

Hsu concedes it is comforting "to know that the God of the universe is good and just and can be trusted to do the right thing." Nevertheless, Hsu insists, "Only God knows the fate of those we grieve."[3]

A word should be said about the growing theological diversity of our world and our neighborhoods. Once upon a time, most Americans had no Hindu neighbors, no Muslim colleagues, no Sikh acquaintances. However, as our world shrinks, some individuals are having difficulty understanding the exclusiveness of Christianity. Diversity will become a major issue of theological dialogue and debate in the years ahead.

In the spirit of compassionate evangelism, my hope is that you, after thoughtful study and reflection, may be able to hear out the concerns of others about the salvation of their beloveds.

Q48   Why do the young die and go to heaven?

Heaven would be pretty dull—and definitely unheavenly—if it were just a group of geezers. In 1924, a minister tried to comfort President Calvin Coolidge after the death of his sixteen-year-old son from blood poisoning. The president silenced him with this observation: "What would Heaven be like if it were made up of only old men and old women?"[1]

Heaven is a party! Who loves parties? Children and adolescents. I know nearly all of us desire a lifespan of "three-score-and-ten," but some people will die young. Yet believe me, they are not short-changed.

If I believe this life is "all there is," then the death of a young adult, an adolescent, a child, a baby is outrageous. But Jesus said, "I come that they may have life, and have it to the full" (John 10:10). I know the real world is beyond death in the eternal timelessness Jesus promised; the party is on the other side.

Q49 My grandson died at sixteen months of age. Will he always be that age in heaven? Will he know me?

I understand why you as a grandparent would ask that. Unfortunately, there is no way to answer this question. I want to believe he will not only know you, he will know how much you loved him. Heaven is timeless, so age does not count in the celestial kingdom. For some, it will be "heaven" to be freed, at last, from the tyranny of age and ageism. My elderly grandfather loved to sing an old gospel song, "Never grow old." I still can hear him sing and see him wipe away tears the last phrase of the chorus, "In a land where we'll never grow old."

You think you have been to some family reunions here. Just wait. I am looking forward to meeting my great-grandfather Charles Wesley Smith, who I have heard so much about. But other great-grandfathers and great-grandmothers will be there too. As will their ancestors. For those interested in genealogy, heaven will be a paradise.

Q50 What about hell? Isn't the concept of hell terribly outdated?

As one who listens to a fair amount of sermons, I cannot remember the last sermon I have heard on hell. Hell is something of an embarrassing doctrine for many in these days of tolerance.

Dozens of expressions contain the word *hell*: "The *hell* you say," "Just for the *hell* of it," "*Hell*, no!" In a sense, the phrases may have evolved as a way to de-claw the awesomeness of hell.

Admittedly, many would agree with theologian Karl Rahner, "As Christians we have to believe hell exists, but we don't have to believe anyone is there."[1]

Actually, the idea of hell is enjoying a resurgence. A 2000 Gallup Poll reports 73 percent of Americans believe in hell, but only 6 percent expect to end up permanent residents (down from 17 percent in 1965).[2] The events of September 11, 2001, have also rekindled a new appreciation for hell. Lots of individuals want a final destination for "really, really evil" individuals.

"Go to hell!" is a common expletive. Actually, if hell exists, that is the worst thing you could ever say to any individual.

Q51   Isn't hell for really evil individuals?

The answer depends on what you mean by "really evil." How many does one have to kill or harm to be "really evil"?

Some people believe, if there is a hell, the best seats are reserved for individuals like Adolph Hitler and Joseph Stalin. Give individuals enough time and they will name candidates who will, as Southerners say, "split hell wide open."

I suspect there will be some "nice" individuals in hell. A couple of my friends believe hell is something of a post-mortem "time out," as in, "You just go to your room and think about what you've done."

I believe hell is for individuals who refuse to honor God's invitation to grace.

Some Christians find it difficult to reconcile hell as eternal punishment with an affirming God "who is loving and merciful and wills all to be saved and forever seeks the loss."[1] If God is

Unconditional Love, how can there be fine print that makes it conditional at the end? My friend Albert Truesdale, a philosopher who has spent a lot of time thinking about hell, wonders, "Can Holy Love ever cease seeking reconciliation without thereby ceasing to be itself?"[2] He goes on to say, "Wherever God is and wherever existence is, whatever exists is the object of active Holy Love. This is the case so long as God is God and so long as anything exists at all."[3] Truesdale further argues, "The Creator would sustain conscious life, not to punish, but to promote reconciliation.[4]

Thus, God's love is continuously at work everywhere in creation: the heavens, earth, *and* hell. Lest that sound too tolerant, consider the psalmist's musing: "Where can I go from your Spirit? Where can I flee from your presence? If I go up to the heavens, you are there; if I make my bed in the depths, you are there" (Psalm 139:7-8).

Q52   Can a Christian believe in reincarnation?

Some Christians are interested in some form of reincarnation as an alternative to the rigid views they have been taught. Others are weighing reincarnation because of exposure to individuals who do believe in the concept.

Morton Kelsey argued that reincarnation is the most widely held view of afterlife, given its foundational status in Buddhism and Hinduism and given the number of adherents in those two faiths.[1] Moreover, both the growth of interest in Asian religions and the increased migration from Asia to the United States have made reincarnation more than an abstract idea for some Western Christians. It is an idea that a colleague, neighbor, or family member might believe. Charles Corr cites the explanation of the Hindu god Krishna:

Wise men do not grieve for the dead or for the living. . . .
Never was there a time when I was not, nor thou . . . nor will

there ever be a time hereafter when we shall cease to be. . . .
Just as a person casts off worn-out garments and puts on others that are new, even so does the embodied soul cast off
worn-out bodies and take on others that are new.[2]

Reincarnationists believe earth is something of a laboratory;
as we repeat life, we learn more and more. If we learn the life lessons, the next life can be better; however, if we fail to learn, the
reincarnation could be a less desirable state of being. Philip
Ruge-Jones notes, "The life you now live is the soul's second
chance (or third, or fourth, or so on). Depending on the life you
live, you may [either] advance or demote the soul's status for its
next trip through the flesh."[3]

While there are Christians who embrace some form of
reincarnation, the concept is in contradiction to the basic
underpinnings of Christianity. Eternal life is not based on anyone's achievements or works; it is a gift of God. Salvation is not
based on our achievements, but on God's graciously outrageous faithfulness.

As I understand reincarnation, one's eternal status is
dependent on what the person does. In Christianity, one's eternal status relies solely on God's gracious gift in Jesus. Paul wrote,
"For it is by grace you have been saved, through faith—and this
not from yourselves, it is the gift of God—not by works, so that
no one can boast" (Ephesians 2:8-9).

The author of Hebrews stated, "Just as man is destined to die
once, and after that to face judgment, so Christ was sacrificed
once to take away the sins of many people" (9:27-28).

I concede that against the threat of hell, the conceptualization of a "second chance" is attractive. However, salvation is a
dynamic process; individuals will continue to grow in holiness,
purity, and intimacy with God. David Ford, writing from an
Orthodox understanding of eternal life, notes, "Sanctification
continues on, in some way, into the world beyond—especially in
the beginning stages of the next life."[4]

I find myself asking why anyone would want to *relive* this life in light of the gracious promise of life eternal with God? Kelsey adds, "If God is as loving and merciful as most of the Christian saints have claimed, and as I have found him to be, it does not seem likely that he wants us to go through the same kind of tasks [or tests] all over again.[5]

Q53   Do other faiths believe in life after death?

Corr, Nabe, and Corr point out that, in all religions, individuals "have sought to find a way to continue after they die what they have found valuable in their lives."[1] They cite the work of R. H. Lifton (1979) on "symbolic immortality." Some will "continue" through offspring; others through their creative efforts in music, books, art, ideas.[2] Thus, some individuals find great substance in linking their lives to those lived by their ancestors.

Any faith, these days, is a loose configuration of ideas. Rarely can we say all Jews, or Christians, or Muslims believe X. Theological perspectives within each religion differ, as do individual beliefs. Here are some broad statements, however.

The goal in Hinduism, through various reincarnations, is an end to the rebirths with an absorption or unity into a transcendent reality. Thus, the ultimate is a state of bliss with Brahman.

In Buddhism, there are two post-life possibilities: some aspect of the human being is reborn, or nirvana or a "blowing out" is achieved. With nirvana, the continuous rebirths end. Nirvana is not heaven. Rather, nirvana "is a condition impossible to describe" that involves serenity and peace.[3]

Islam has strong concepts about eternal life. One's actions, good and bad are recorded in The Book of Deeds. After death, Allah appraises the record and an individual will either go to heaven or to hell. Then, John Esposito explains, "The pleasures of heaven and the pain of hell will be fully experienced."[4] Heaven is a paradise of "perpetual peace and bliss with flowing rivers, beautiful gardens, and the enjoyment of one's spouses (multiple marriage partners are permitted in Islam). More controversial, these days, are the *houris*—the beautiful, dark-eyed female companions[5] seemingly promised to martyrs.

From a Jewish and Christian perspective, the wisdom writing of Ecclesiastes insists that God "set eternity in the hearts of men; yet they cannot fathom what God has done from beginning to end" (3:11).

Yet some of my Jewish friends believe in eternal life, and some don't. Each individual has to reconcile his or her own beliefs. Arthur O. Roberts wondered:

> I've kept my life as a scientist and as a believer
> separate for years. But my wife died last month
> and now I'm trying to put the compartments together.
> My head says she is just ashes strewn at sea.
> But my heart tells me Martha lives, somewhere.
> Help me sort it out, Lord.[6]

10. Questions about Grief and Communication

"I also grew up at a time when you didn't talk about it.
I'd think, I know somebody just died, but nobody's
talking about it, so I better not talk about it either.
Even though I knew the whole world was talking about it."
—*Maria Shriver*[1]

Q54 No one in my late husband's family talks about the big "D" subject. How can I get them to talk about his death?

This is a common predicament in families where many chose to keep their grief "close" to themselves. Unfortunately, family members have stories and details of a life that need to be shared, particularly with children.

Most people know the saying, "There's an elephant in the room." The "elephant" is an issue people are unwilling to discuss. How can anyone ignore an elephant? In some families, ignoring uncomfortable issues becomes an art form.

Here are three steps I would suggest:

- Raise the issue of your husband's death and keep raising the issue.
- Audit the family to identify someone who is the most receptive to the possibility of conversation and supporting your openness.
- Talk. By talking you may lead to a "talking it over" or a "talking it out."

In his powerful memoir, *The Blessing*, Greg Orr reveals that his family "shut down" after he accidentally shot his brother while hunting. During his grief, Orr discovered his father, when he about Greg's age, had shot and killed a friend in a hunting accident. Unfortunately, his father and his aunt had not spoken since the accident. The silence produced incredible suffering for Orr.[1]

Ignoring elephants won't make them go away. Keep trying to encourage conversation.

Q55 I get angry when individuals tell me my daughter is in heaven and "with Jesus." I want her here! What should I tell them?

For some grievers, believing their loved ones are "with Jesus" is comforting. For others, the idea is like a pebble in the shoe or nails across a chalkboard.

Some grieving individuals are card-carrying members of the "Association of Nice Grievers." Their motto is to be polite no matter what anyone says to them, however insensitive. Others belong to the "Association of Take Their Heads Off Grievers," who show no mercy. Those who say something insensitive or stupid will pay dearly.

Some belong to the "Association of Tutorial Grievers." When someone says something unkind or insensitive, they seize the opportunity to turn it into an educational moment. "Let me tell you how that sounds to me." Actually, if more individuals belonged to this group, there would be fewer insensitive things said.

"People mean well" is a cliché used to explain away others' insensitive words and actions. Unfortunately, these individuals will keep on "meaning well" unless someone challenges them. Just be careful that, in your anger over your daughter's physical absence, you don't alienate yourself or drive away her presence in your memories.

Q56 When individuals ask me how I am doing, I generally respond "fine." If I share how I really am coping, it only makes them uncomfortable. Should I always honestly tell individuals how I am feeling?

In many situations where we wish to be polite, we edit our responses and are selective with whom we share our true feelings. Grievers find that friends fall into two groups: those to whom you can talk honesty and those to whom you cannot.

Many individuals are anxious around you because they are afraid of saying the wrong thing or something that will hurt you. Most individuals who have not experienced gut-ripping grief want to believe that grievers "get over it and move on." They want to believe that in no time at all, a griever can be "fine."

When approached by someone with this query, ask yourself: "Does this person really want to know or are they asking to be polite?" One grieving father told me that individuals soon stopped asking "How are you?" because they did not want to hear he was having a tough time with his child's death. Instead, they complimented him. "You are doing so well. I don't know what I would do if I lost a child." Moreover, they never hung around after the compliment.

This could be your moment to do a tutorial: "If you would like to know, and if you have time to listen, I would be happy to tell you. I am struggling. I am having good days and bad days. I am having a hard time believing that (name of loved one) is dead." Remember, someday the questioner will be on the other side of the question. Your honesty might give them insight and the courage to be honest.

Q57 Why do individuals use so many clichés about grief?

We fall back on clichés because we are a death-denying culture. Unfortunately, some individuals can "string" clichés and fill the air with words. But their words are like cotton candy—without nutritional substance. If David Letterman had a "Top Ten" list of clichés, these would be on it:

~ "God never gives us more that we can handle."

~ "She/he is in a better place."

~ "God took your loved one to be a flower in his bouquet."

~ "It's not for us to ask why."

~ "It's all for the best."

~ "Time heals the hurt."

As Adin Steinsaltz points out, clichés are shorthand, or "fillers" in conversational flow.[1] I am surprised more individuals are not pummeled severely about the head and shoulders after a string of clichés. What the ancient griever Job observed three thousand years ago sums it up in one word: worthless. Job, after the death of his ten children and barraged with "comfort" from three insensitive friends, observed, "Does not the ear test words as the tongue tastes food?" (Job 12:11).

Q58 My son thinks that if he talks about his father, it will make me sad. How do I change his mind?

Understandably, you probably cried or were emotional when you first talked with your child about the death. Your child sees that, in your grief, you are "different" than you were before, and your reactions may be more unpredictable. Because your son wants predictability in what he has learned is an unpredictable world, he may be editing his conversations to avoid a reaction.

Or possibly someone told your son to "be strong for your mother." Or that he may need to be "the man" of the house. Lots of children, of all ages, have been told similar phrases. The children sometimes react by putting on the equivalent of an emotional suit of armor. Following the death of her husband, Coretta Scott King created tension between her children when she told Martin III that he was "the head of the house now." In his brother Dexter's words, "Martin took it to heart . . . with him suddenly trying to be the man, with no model."[1]

Let your son know his reserve or "strongness" troubles you. If possible, talk to him. Or write him a note or an e-mail. Begin with a sentence like, "I need to tell you how I am hearing your silence about your father's death." Tell him the silence hurts more. It is his father's death, not talking about it, that makes you sad.

Q59 My sixteen-year-old is acting weird since her father's death. If I ask how she is feeling, she says, "Fine. I am fine." But she is not talking to me. She spends so much time at her computer. How can I get her to talk to me?

Sometimes it is difficult to distinguish adolescent grief expression from normal adolescent communication difficulties. Adolescents do not want anything to make them different from their peers. Nothing makes them more different like a death of a family member, particularly if there is any stigma attached to it. The more grief changes the home environment or economic framework, the more challenging communication may be.

Some teens may have had a tense relationship with the deceased but now selectively recall and edit memories. Some may feel real guilt about the relationship. "Should haves" careen the corridors of adolescent minds.

It is possible the time she spends at the computer is her "safe place" to grieve. You might want to try communicating with her through e-mail.

Q60 Our baby daughter died almost a year ago. No one ever asks how I, the father, am doing. Everyone asks, "How is your wife doing?" How can I tell individuals I am grieving too?

A lot of grief assessment is influenced by cultural baggage about gender roles. The cultural myth surrounding a perinatal loss is that fathers do not grieve. Or that they do not grieve as much as mothers. Admittedly, biological mothers may be more emotionally and physiologically attached since they carried the baby. Some fathers do not develop a sense of attachment until after the baby is born. But that does not excuse the insensitivity of your friends.

You may want to respond, "Thank you for asking about my wife. Would you like to know how I am doing?"

Q61 Everyone tells me, "Be strong!" What does that mean? Does that mean I am never to acknowledge my grief?

You grieve in a "get-over-it" and "move-on-with-it" world. Some families—or family members—have strong expectations for emotional control. The suggestion to "be strong" usually means to confine your grief to private spaces. Some individuals are afraid of emotions; hence, they invest great energy in maintaining the appearance of "being strong."

Historically, it has been considered more important for males to be strong. If I had a dollar for every time a male is told, "Be strong," I would be wealthy. The phrase communicates, "Buck up" and "Suck up" the pain, or in other words, "Take it like a man!"

Martin Luther, following the death of his daughter, rebuked his sixteen-year-old son Hans. Hans wanted to come home from boarding school to be with the family (he had come home for the funeral then returned to school). Luther informed the school's headmaster, "As a result of the death of his sister and especially of the conversations with his mother, my son has become weak-hearted. But he must not give in to his sentiments, and he cannot come home, or he will never become a real man."[1]

Luther was more demanding with Hans: "Do your best to master your tears like a man, and be careful not to give your mother pain again and not to make her anxious about you . . . she wants you to master your sorrow and to study cheerfully and quietly."[2] Hans did not come home.

Not "being strong" is thought by some to be an embarrassment. In his memoirs, President George H. Bush wrote about his plane being shot down during World War II. Two of his crew did not survive.

There were no signs of Del or Ted anywhere around. I looked as I floated down and afterwards kept my eye open from the raft, but to no avail. The fact that our planes didn't seem to be searching anymore showed me pretty clearly that they had not gotten out. I'm afraid I was pretty much of a sissy about it cause I sat in my raft and sobbed for a while. It bothers me so very much. [3]

Decades later, Bush's mother, Dorothy Walker Bush, died. It happened just two weeks after losing the election to Bill Clinton. The former president noted the death in his journal:

Mum left us. It's kind of like our compass is spinning a little. Even when she was tired and failing she was our guide. I walked by the Bungalow [her cottage in the Kinnebuckport compound] a lot this long Thanksgiving weekend. I found myself choking up. Then I found myself smiling. The [Secret Service] agents probably said to each other, "The old guy's finally lost it." But I couldn't help but think of the happy things and the sad things, but always at the center was Mum, stable, loving, kind, generous, thinking of the other guy.[4]

"Be strong" is a euphemism that means to deny or hide your grief because it makes others uncomfortable.

The need to appear "strong" sometimes limits acts of compassion. Bush declined the invitation to give the eulogy for his best friend, C. Fred Chambers, because he was not sure he could keep control of his emotions. He wrote the widow, "I hope I haven't let you down by not speaking in tribute to C. Fred."[5]

Historically women did not attend funerals or, if they attended the funeral, they did not attend the committal because they were thought to be "too weak." Mary Todd Lincoln did not attend the funerals of either of her sons, Edward who died in 1849 or Willie who died in 1863. Nor did she go to the funeral of her husband, President Abraham Lincoln, in 1865.

Increasingly, these days, women are expected to "be strong" and not to "go to pieces."

Joe Gargan, Caroline Kennedy Schlossberg's cousin, praised Caroline after the death of her brother, John F. Kennedy Jr.: "She is like a rock. She knows John would want her to pick up and move on with her life."[6]

In the admonition, "*Be strong,*" some hear an exclamation mark. With more women in the workplace, where any open display of grief is discouraged or a threat to "the team spirit," more women are hearing, "Be strong." Unfortunately, "*Be strong*" sounds like the words Archie Bunker barked at Edith, "Would you stifle yourself!"

How should you respond to the cliché? Here are three suggestions:

- *Be direct.* Too many grievers are too polite; this will only lead to another griever being told these same words. I suggest you say, "Would you like to know how the words 'be strong' sound to me at this point in my life?"
- *Be creative.* Sit down and repeat the words "be strong" several times, then try to compose a poem using the phrase. Something you write could give encouragement to another griever.
- *Be human.* Authentic human beings grieve and acknowledge grief. They will not go along with the "be strong" mantra simply to make others feel less uncomfortable. By not "being strong," you may help start a revolution and give others permission, in their own grieving seasons, not to feel the need to fake strength.
- *Forgive yourself and others.* If you do simply ignore the words, do not stew over them or rehearse "I should have saids." Let it go.

Q62 My grief as a grandparent gets overlooked. When my grandchild died, I was so concerned about how my daughter and son-in-law were taking it, I discounted my own grief. How can I communicate I am grieving too?

Grandparents often experience a double-edged grief: They grieve for the grandchild, and they also grieve for their son or daughter. Therese Rando comments: "[Grandparents] not only lose their grandchild, but they 'lose' their child as well, as they cannot rescue their child from bereaved-parent status."[1]

"The burden is a long-lasting one," says Mary Lou Reed, who has researched the grieving experience of grandparents. "Even grandparents who found some feelings of 'peace' about the death of their grandchild frequently mention that the pain they see in their own child over the years is a never-ending source of sorrow."[2]

Older grandparents sometimes experience an intense angst: "Why didn't God take me? I've lived my life. Her/his life was just beginning! She/he had life ahead of them."

Reed identifies two barrier myths that prevent people from reaching out to grandparents. First, some people believe that because the loss is "one generation removed," grandparents should be immune from intense pain. Second, some people think that since grandparents are older, they are more experienced in coping with death.[3]

Well-wishers often fail to support grandparents in their suffering.

I have been amazed by some grandparents' faith and resourcefulness. I also know there are those wondering moments when their "whys" flow like flood waters down a dry creek bed. Or when fatigue exacerbates their grief, especially for those who are dealing with multiple losses. Too many grandparents take on the "be strong" role for the entire family. That can be pulled off publicly, but in private the effort and the anguish can be soul-killing.

I've thought a great deal about grandparents' grief because of the number of grandparents rearing grandchildren. Indeed, some grandparents must put their own grief on hold because, due to the death of an adult son or daughter, or due to other unfortunate circumstances, they have now become the caregivers for their grandchildren. A 2003 study reports that 5.8 million grandparents have grandchildren living with them; 2.4 million are the primary caregivers.[4] This night, long after you have shut this book, a grandparent will be going the second or twenty-second mile, perhaps mumbling, "I am too old to be doing this." Nevertheless, they will offer what a grandchild needs: an anchor.

Where does a grandparent go to grieve? What can a grandparent do?

- ↝ *Find someone to talk to.* Seek out other grandparents, counselors, pastors, or close friends. Acknowledge the double-edged grief you are experiencing.
- ↝ *Step forward as you are able.* Sometimes, the grandparent must advocate for the good of the whole family. A son or daughter may be so paralyzed by grief that they neglect their other children. This can lead to situations ripe for misunderstanding. Sometimes we need to ask what is best for each grandchild.
- ↝ *Seize the opportunities for a special time for bonding with grandchildren.* A grieving grandchild may ask grandparents questions they cannot take to a parent. Many grandparents have, in grief, become a source of stability and unconditional love.

Q63 All my life I have been somebody's "something." Now I am alone and am nobody's "nothing." We had no children. How do I find a new identity?

David Wolpe relates a story about an elderly woman being interviewed about the difficulties of aging, particularly after so many friends had died. The interviewer asked what she missed the most. "There is no one to call me Rosie anymore."[1]

Your question is often reflected in the music of our culture. Frank Sinatra sang, "Everybody Needs Somebody, Sometime." Desiring and enjoying relationships is part of human nature. Perhaps you remember Sonny and Cher's rendition of "I've Got You, Babe."

Yet it is possible to so immerse ourselves in a role that we lose our own personhood. Mothers, for example, often pour themselves into their children. Their sense of identity can become tied to their children. Similarly, spouses—or life partners—often develop a "joint persona." Belonging to each other, while beneficial, creates dependence.

Robert Neimeyer observed that death and loss "tear the vital strands of connection that define who we are, and we only effortfully and gradually repair them by reestablishing other forms of connection to that which we had lost."[2]

In a real sense, the death of a spouse gives us custody of ourselves. For some, the thought is frightening. For others, it may be liberating. I have worked with women who married immediately out of high school or even before graduation. These women moved from a bedroom in a parent's home into a bedroom in a husband's apartment. In widowhood, some find an independence never before experienced.

The task is to be a good steward of "me." We do that by periodically auditing our lives with this question, "Who am I *now*?" Many individuals need to explore their "now-ness" in a mutual help group or in counseling.

II. Questions about the Death of a Parent

"You never really feel alone in the world
until you stand on your parent's grave."
—*Gary Small*[1]

"It seems that my basic role in the universe has changed.
I am no longer anyone's child; I must now assume the adult
place at the family table and in the family portrait.
How can that be? I'm not ready! There is still so much
to learn, so many mistakes to make."
—*Darcie Sims*[2]

Q64 I know that someday I will lose my
mother—who is my best friend. She is
always there for me. How will I live
without her?

Increasingly, this is a challenge to be faced in our culture as individuals live longer. One hundred years ago, you would have been hard pressed to find someone who would identify a mother as a "best friend." Smaller families have also shaped this relational reality.

However, you need to practice imagining your life after your mother's death, because in all probability, she will die before you. Spend these years investing in conversations and activities that will create a well-stocked memory resource. Some would say, "Enjoy your mother while you can."

Q65 Since my father died, my brother has been trying to take dad's place. As executor, he wants to make decisions and have everyone go along with him. I had one dad and do not need another. How do I tell him without making him angry?

Upon the death of a father, legions of males, of all ages, have been told "You are the man of the family now." Or "It's up to you!" Even if no one said these specific words to your brother, he may have heard this indirectly through some individuals' attempts at conversation and comfort.

Some adult children take a "got to get this done" approach to executorship. They sense it as an obligation rather than a gift to the family. Clearly, considering it as a gift is better. I have been grateful to my nephew for his faithful stewardship of the responsibility of serving as executor of my mother's estate.

If you're unhappy with the way your brother has taken the helm, you need to say so. But realize by challenging his "coup" of leadership, you could make him angry. On the other hand, he may not have wanted this role in the first place; some men accept the challenge willingly while others muddle through. Your brother may welcome sharing responsibility rather than have the whole responsibility.

Some families have rigid concepts about masculine leadership in times of crisis.

Find a time to talk to him about your concerns. You need to have reflected, and perhaps rehearsed, what you want to say to him and what you hope he will hear. Before voicing your concerns, find some detail to compliment him on. Point out that you are not attacking him, but you want more family consensus in decision-making.

If you are female, keep in mind stereotypical attitudes. One middle-aged woman, the "baby" of the family who had never married, became resentful about her brother taking her deceased's father's place and telling her, from time to time, what she "should" do. A T-shirt she wore to the family reunion communicated her feelings: "I AM NOBODY'S BABY, ANYMORE!"

Q66 I am a grown adult with grandchildren. Although my mother died a long, long time ago, I still have periods when I miss her deeply. Is this abnormal?

You may keenly miss a loved one from an older generation because there is now no relative to be a "barrier" between you and death. Or your mother's death may have made you part of the older generation before you are ready to be part of that generation. Sometimes, we miss an elder's encouragement, wisdom, sense of "knowing what to do" in particular situations or their confidence in us. We also miss the influence the elder would have had with children or grandchildren.

There is no "statute of limitations" on missing and remembering. I am more concerned about individuals who seemingly "get over it" easily, who do not miss loved ones.

Q67 How do I help a parent who has lost a mate when he lives far away from me?

In the summer of 2003, thousands of French elders died during the heat wave that struck Paris and surrounding communities. Ironically, one paragraph in the newspaper account continues to trouble me: "Many victims died alone in overheated city apartments while their families were away on vacation." One young adult, Celine Rocquain, lamented "Paris is the capital of individualism. A small gesture could have saved many of them." How could so many elders have had no one checking in on them?[1]

Given the mobility of the nation (one in five Americans moves every decade) "long-distance" caregiving, or concern-making, is often the norm. Many individuals use vacation days not to rest but to check up on an aged parent or relative.

Here are some ideas to consider:

Keep in touch. Take the phone commercial "reach out and touch someone" to heart. Listen not only to the words but also to how it is said and to what is not said. Listen for slurred speech that suggests the parent is confused or intoxicated.

Develop an area code ally. Find someone in your parent's area code or community who can be your "eyes" and "ears." When you call a grieving parent, everything may be fine. However, the local person may drop in and notice uneaten food or disheveled clothing. Do not consider this to be "spying" on a parent.

Offer to monitor or manage the parent's checking accounts. There are individuals who would take advantage of a grieving elder—some, unfortunately, are family members. Be on the lookout for large unexplained cash withdraws.

Ask to be included in decisions about major household expenditures. Some unscrupulous contractors prey on the elderly—particularly if they were not accustomed to managing home repairs.

Go online and check for bereavement groups in your parent's neighborhood or community.

Keep phone numbers and e-mail addresses for neighbors or friends who can, in an emergency, check in with your parent.

Expect some resistance from a parent. No one, these days, wants to grow old or dependent. Your grieving parent may fuss but, inwardly, be pleased by your concern.

12. Questions about the Death of a Child

"People say losing a child is the worst. I know of nothing
more accurate. It's like joining a club you don't want
to belong to—and you're in it for life."
—*Howard Twitty*[1]

"I hated that nobody mentioned her;
it was as if she had never been.
I know now it was because
our friends did not want to hurt us,
but you don't think too clearly after a death."
—*Barbara Bush*[2]

"Burying infants, we bury the future,
unwieldy and unknown, full of promise
and possibilities, outcomes punctuated by our rosy hopes.
The grief has no borders, no limits, no known ends,
and the little infant graves that edge the corners
and fencerows of every cemetery are
never quite big enough to contain that grief."
—*Thomas Lynch*[3]

Q68 Are couples who have a child die more likely to divorce?

The relationship between death of a child and divorce has become an urban legend in our culture. Barbara Bush, in her memoirs, reported the divorce rate for grieving parents is 70 percent.[1] That statistic, however, is not supported by solid research but anecdotal reports. Because percentages are often tossed about as a fact, I fear the statistics become something of a self-fulfilling prophecy.

After a thorough review of psychological studies, Mark Hardt and Danette Carroll reported divorce rates range from the low of 25 percent to the high of 90 percent, so "it is commonly assumed that the death of a child serves also as a death knell to the marriage of affected parents."[2]

Hardt and Carroll found a radically lower divorce rate. Out of 147 parents, only eleven reported divorcing, or separating, after the death of a child—7.5 percent. Admittedly, 29 percent acknowledged that they had *thought* about divorce or separation. These researchers concluded, "For couples who have lost a child, it is important that divorce does not appear to be the inevitable outcome that it has long been assumed."[3]

A team of respected researchers led by Shirley A. Murphy re-examined findings of more than one hundred studies and found data in only two studies that demonstrated higher divorce rates among bereaved parents than nonbereaved couples. In a study of forty-six couples five years after the death of a child, Murphy found that only 9 percent had divorced. Murphy concludes that "rates of divorce among bereaved parents have been highly and falsely inflated."[4]

In reality, the death of the child *can* be the "final straw" for already troubled or dysfunctional marriages. It becomes a way "out" of the marriage and to dodge the pain. Admittedly, if parents do not communicate, one parent may turn to an outside party to "acknowledge" the anguish of the grief and the strain on the marriage. Some of these conversations lead to affairs. If auditory intimacy leads to sexual intimacy, the marriage will be challenged.

Dick Gilbert, director of the World Pastoral Care Center concedes, "Clearly, marriages change even if the couple does not divorce."[5] Almost forty years after the death of her three-year-old son, Ikky, First Lady Mamie Eisenhower told a reporter, "Giving up a baby is the hardest trial a young couple may have to face" because the loss makes the couple significantly different than peers.[6] Biographer Carlo D'Este added:

> Ikky's death left a permanent scar on both parents. Somehow they pretended to cope but fooled no one. Instead of drawing closer together in the wake of Ikky's death, each retreated into a private world of sorrow and suffered in silence, their only common bond their beloved son's death.[7]

Conversely, shared suffering can draw a couple together. On August 9, 1963, two-day-old Patrick Bouvier Kennedy died of complications from hyaline membrane disease. The nation's heart went out to the grieving First Family. Although he was president, John F. Kennedy rearranged his schedule to spend twenty-three days in isolation with Jackie, Caroline, and John. What an example to grieving parents that was. Aides and friends witnessed a new closeness between the couple. Jackie and John Kennedy had had a troubled marriage, a fact that was not known extensively during his presidency.[8] Jackie told her friend, decorator Billy Baldwin, "It took a very long time for us to work everything out, but we did, and we were about to have a real life together."[9] Patrick's death brought them together. But 104 days later, Jackie Kennedy would be grieving for the president himself.

Parental grievers want someone to listen to them and to acknowledge their pain. Unfortunately, too many people lean on clichés and assumptions for comfort: "Oh, you are young. You can have another baby." Such responses short-circuit honest pain expression. A healthy marital narrative must integrate the death of a child.

Q69 I think my children are handling their sister's death as well as can be expected. What are some long-term consequences for children who lose a sibling?

The death of a sibling and the parents' reaction to the death of a sibling can be a significant shaping influence on a child's life. First, the death and grief make the child different than peers. Second, grief changes the environment in which the child lives. In essence, a child looses both a sibling *and* the comfortable home environment—both of which are significant losses that must be mourned.

A third effect is that, in some cases, a child may lose childhood innocence. In 1953, seven-year-old George W. Bush, "took care" of his mother, Barbara, for some months after the death of his four-year-old sister Robin. One biographer identified Robin's death as one of the shaping events of the president's life. In his autobiography, *A Charge to Keep*, the president himself wrote, "Forty-six years later, those minutes remain the starkest memory of my childhood, a sharp pain in the midst of an otherwise happy blur."[1] He reflected, "I guess I learned at an early age, never to take life for granted. But rather than making me fearful, the close reach of death made me determined, determined to enjoy whatever life might bring, to live each day to the fullest."[2]

Children will grieve intermittently and need to be allowed to be children. Children need to be able to ask their questions or voice observations about the death. After Robin's death, George

If it is difficult for you as an adult to find words to describe your feelings, how much more so for a child.

W. Bush's father took him to a football game in Midland, Texas. At some point, son George groaned, "Boy, I wish I was with Robin." A stunned father asked, "Why do you say that?" The son responded, "I bet she can see the game better from up there than we can from here."[3]

Unfortunately, some children assume or create some sense of responsibility for the death, particularly if they had tension or intense rivalry with the deceased sibling. The danger unfolds when children conclude they have to make it up to the parents. Or when children are told, "You have to be good and not bother your parents/mother/father."

Susan Sonnenday Vogel, following the death of her son Mark, feared her younger son David would sense a need to become "the replacement." She broached that concern by writing David, "It is my fear that you will believe that you must take Mark's place and your own as well. I fear that you will feel you have to make up for the loss by being more than you are.[4]

No family has been more affected by the "replacement" syndrome than the Kennedys. The patriarch, Ambassador Joseph Kennedy, had sweeping political aspirations for his oldest son, Joseph Jr. When Joe died in World War II, the father transferred those dreams onto the next oldest, John. One wonders what might John have become had his brother lived.

Q70 Is it really possible to "replace" a child?

No. However, for centuries, physicians (and family members and pastors) often urged couples have another child as soon as possible. In 1528, Martin and Katherine Luther, following the death of eight-month-old Elizabeth, became devoted to Magdalene, who was conceived soon after Elizabeth's death. The Luthers "interpreted her birth as a consolation for the death of the little girl taken from them so quickly."[1]

Franklin and Eleanor Roosevelt had two children named Franklin *Junior*. The first Franklin, who lived to be just eight months old, died in 1909. Mrs. Roosevelt became pregnant again, and they named the next child Franklin as well. The second Franklin lived to adulthood. In Mrs. Roosevelt's day, it was commonly believed another pregnancy could be a satisfactory distraction from the grief.

Today, physicians and family members are more likely to revere each individual life and encourage parents to take the time to grieve. Each child, living or dead, is special.

Q 71   Our first child, a son, died. Two years later we had another son. How much should we tell him about his brother?

Much like the issue of sexuality, information should be age and comprehension appropriate. Initially, you may choose to show pictures of the deceased sibling. Remember, a child can learn about a deceased brother or sister in lots of ways.

Dawn Siegrist Waltman made the decision to talk freely with her other children about her child born dead. She commented, "Although my children never saw Molly alive, there was no denying that they loved and cherished their baby sister. Their notes and crayon drawings clearly reflected that." Waltman bought helium-filled balloons for each member of the family. She asked each to write or draw a "birthday" message. Those notes or drawings were tied to the balloon strings and the balloons were released.

Waltman concedes, "To the person looking in from the outside, this whole activity may have seemed silly or even a waste of time." However, the family project "generated memories and conversations about Molly's life in my womb and her life now in heaven."[1] It "jump-started" many future conversations.

It should be acknowledged that not every family member might choose to participate in a commemorative event. Talk over plans ahead of time. Give individuals a chance to ponder options. Realistically, some family members or friends may challenge your decision. But if it works for you and your family, then invest in the experience.

Realize that your child's awareness could create interest, confusion, tension, or misunderstanding with friends or the parents of friends. Waltman recalls that after the balloon release on her child's birthday, her son Matthew yelled to his neighbor pal, "Shawn, guess what? We just wished my baby sister 'Happy birthday!' and guess where she lives? In heaven!"[2]

Q72 We had a child die before we moved here. How should we answer the question, "How many children do you have?"

Many parents would answer, "It depends." Will the individual asking the question become uncomfortable with the answer if you are honest? Some parents practice so they can answer without hesitating. One friend says, "I have one son in Kansas and one son in heaven."

John Dasberg, former CEO of Burger King and Northwest Airlines, had a six-year-old daughter who died. For a time, he put away her picture in his office. Then he returned her picture to his desk—beside the pictures of his two living children—an action that made a few visitors and colleagues uncomfortable. He explained his decision, "I don't want to deny her memory. To say that I have two children is denying that she was here for six years."[1]

13. Questions about Children and Grief

"Children's questions should be answered in a straightforward direct fashion, and in terms of the family's shared beliefs regarding family roles, separation, death or the afterlife. . . . If children are old enough to formulate questions about these losses, they are old enough to deserve appropriate answers."
—*Robert A. Neimeyer*[1]

Q73 Is it wise to shield a child from death and grief?

How can a child be shielded from death and grief these days? Still, disclosure should be proportional. Talk about death with the cautious intention you would use in talking about sex.

Take the child's maturation level into consideration. The Kennedy clan gathered the night of the president's funeral and burial to celebrate young John's third birthday. They sensed that even though John could not comprehend his father's death, he did understand a birthday party. Children are curious and need permission to ask questions. They need truthful, if careful, answers.

Whenever one fictionalizes answers, or evades the question, eventually the child learns the truth and trust will be challenged.

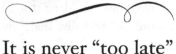

It is never "too late" to help a child do grief work.

Listen to the child with your eyes as well as your ears. What is the child really asking? Am I safe? Are you going to die too? What is going to happen to me? Identify who else the child is asking and what those answers may be. Too many children perceive that their questions make adults uncomfortable and begin editing the questions or going to other sources for answers.

One adult recalled a sibling's death, "But no one talked about it much; the 1950s were a time when a death or any other tragedy in a family was viewed as just that: personal. I didn't know that of course. I was only seven."[1] In too many families, these words are as still true as when George W. Bush experienced them.

Helen Fitzgerald suggests a simple conversation starter: "Kelly, I remember how upset you were when Charlie died. It was a terrible time for both of us. I wonder if we could talk about it?" The parent needs to know what the child knows—and fears—and then "fill in the gaps." Moreover, says Fitzgerald, "It might even be appropriate to share with her the reasons why you made certain decisions concerning the extent of her involvement."[2] Build a framework for future conversations. "Kelly, I want us to be able to talk about this anytime, okay?"

Q74 How much do children comprehend about death?

Historically, children were not shielded from death. Because most adults died not in hospitals but at home, children were more aware of death than children today.

Even so, children today understand more than adults assume. Admittedly, their awareness is based on the level of emotional and intellectual maturity of the child. All children immediately comprehend that their environment has changed or is changing. The child realizes, "My mommy cries all the time," or "My dad is sad and doesn't want to play with me."

Children need encouragement to ask their questions and to expect honest, accurate answers. If it has been difficult for you to comprehend a death, imagine what it must be like for a child to deal with it and verbalize his or her feelings. Information must be given in terms the child can understand. When ten-year-old Rosie was told that her mother had died of hepatitis, she went to a library and looked up the word: "a disease associated with needles." She concluded her mother had died from complications of sewing.[1]

Children may be concerned with who will die next. Or that a parent will die. Children often have difficulty comprehending the permanence of death. Days after the death of President John F. Kennedy, three-year-old John Jr. asked to talk to Evelyn Lincoln, his father's private secretary. During the phone call, when John told her he wanted to come and visit, she replied that a visit would be nice. At the end of the conversation, young John stunned the secretary by asking, "Mrs. Lincoln, is my father there?"[2]

Children are sensitive to body language and verbal discomfort of adults. Many can sense partial truths. Children also compare answers and responses for cohesion in the narrative. To aid a child's comprehension of the loss, it is important that there be a shared understanding among those talking to a child about a death—parents, grandparents, siblings, teachers, friends, and companions.

Q75 How old should a child be to attend a funeral?

A parent must decide in light of the emotional maturity of the child. Ask a child if she or he would like to attend. Really, no one is comfortable at a funeral. Alan Wolfelt comments: "Since the funeral of someone loved is a significant event, children should have the same opportunity to attend as any other member of the family. That's 'allowed' to attend, not 'forced.'"[1]

Children can be more comfortable if prepared for a funeral or memorial service. Give a child an idea of what to expect: name some individuals who will attend, explain that some individuals will be crying, describe a casket or urn. For some children a memorial service may be easier since there is no body present.

How long a child stays is just as important. Increasingly, many funeral homes are providing "children's rooms" where a child can draw, read books, or watch a video.

Q76 How do I explain death to a child?

Start with trying to explain this particular death rather than death in general. Then gear your discussion of "what is death" to the child's level of understanding.

I use a glove to show that the glove is lifeless without a hand inside. Then I put the glove on and begin moving it. "Look at all the things this glove can do. It can snap fingers, it can pinch, it can pick up things. Why? Because of the hand *inside* the glove." Then I peel off the glove. "See how lifeless it is again? The glove now cannot touch or pinch or hold. After death, our bodies are like this glove. What made us unique is the spirit *inside* our bodies."

Answering a child's questions is not always easy. Sometimes, adults have wondered or are wondering the same questions. Do not attempt to "control" the discussion.

Q77 How should I respond when my child asks, "Are you going to die too?"

It is more important that you answer questions comfortably rather than the words you use. Do not answer in a way that diminishes the child's curiosity in asking. Children quickly sense adult discomfort and conclude, "Mustn't ask that again."

Sometimes the timing of the question is not convenient. So parents offer a temporary answer but promise a more detailed response later. In a safer time or place, revisit the question.

Parents need to realize that some may answer a child's questions more bluntly or with theological perspectives that make them uncomfortable. In one family, following the death of an adult son, a son-in-law informed his son, the deceased's eight-year-old nephew, that he had died and gone to hell. (Factually, he had died with complications from AIDS). The mother of the child (the sister of the deceased) did not discover this until one night when she found her child sobbing. "What's the matter?" Through wracking sobs the boy answered, "Uncle Ed is in hell."

Admittedly the father believed that his brother-in-law had gone to hell based on his interpretation of certain Scriptures. His wisdom, however, in sharing that perspective with a child was questionable.

Q78 Sometimes, my seven-year-old says he wishes he could die so he could live with his father in heaven. What should I tell him?

Children have only a limited vocabulary to capture their emotions following a death. This child really does not want to die but wants to see his father. You might respond, "You know, it's natural. Sometimes, I wish I could just go to heaven and see him too. Someday, we will see him again. And he will be so glad to see you. But in the meantime, we can remember all the good times we had with him." You might want to compare the waiting to Christmas or to a birthday or to summer vacation at the beach.

You also might ask, "Can you remember a good time we had together?" Or you may want to prod the child's memory, "Do you remember the time we went to the beach?" This is a great time to have (or create) a special photo album for the child. "Let's look at some of the pictures so we can remember the fun times we had together."

14. Questions about Suicide

"When the suicide bomb drops, however,
one group of people is always standing
at ground zero: the members of the surviving family."
—*John H. Hewett*[1]

Q79 Is suicide on the increase or are we just more open to talk about it today?

Suicide is a significant issue in American culture. On average, eighty-one individuals end their lives by suicide every day. A total of 29,359 Americans committed suicide in 2000. More individuals die yearly from suicide than from homicide. Suicide is the eleventh-leading cause of death among Americans.[1]

Suicide receives intense media attention when celebrity or public figures like Kurt Cobain, Admiral Michael Broda, or Pulitzer Prize-winning author Lewis Puller Jr. take their own lives.

Q8o Why are so many adolescents committing suicide?

Suicide is the third-leading cause of death for young adults. In numbers, some five thousand Americans between the ages of fifteen and twenty-four die by suicide each year. Between 1952 and 1995, the incidence of suicide among adolescents tripled. Between 1980 and 1996, the incidence of suicide among African-American males, ages fifteen to nineteen, increased 105 percent![1]

The Centers for Disease Control identifies contagion as a significant factor: The exposure "to the suicide or suicidal behavior of one or more persons influences others to commit suicide,"[2] especially in light of the widespread media attention to a suicide by a celebrity, particularly when technical details about the method are included in the coverage. Unfortunately, too many adolescents perceive suicide as a "means of coping with personal problems" such as the break-up of a relationship or retaliation against parental discipline. The CDC also identifies "an increasing interaction of risk factors," such as substance abuse, mental illness, a history of violence and family disruption, severe stress in social and school life, and rapid sociological change.

Howard Schubiner, a physician who has called for more attention to adolescents' mental health during a visit to a physician, identifies "adolescents who have recently suffered a real or perceived loss" as at high risk.[3] He argues that more attention must be paid to medical and emotional issues of adolescents. A study by the Substance Abuse and Mental Health Services Administration reported that close to three million adolescents, ages twelve to seventeen, "considered" suicide in 2000, and one-third of those attempted to end their lives. Outrageously, "only one in three of those who reported considering suicide or trying to kill themselves received counseling."[4]

Some statistics report that gay, lesbian, and bisexual adolescents have higher rates of suicidal ideation. They attempt suicide at rates three times higher than heterosexual adolescents and "may account for as many as 30 percent of the completed youth suicides each year."[5] Early and middle adolescents are significantly less able to cope with the isolation and stigma of a sexual identity that is initially acknowledged as being "different than peers" and the accompanying—or feared—discrimination and loss of friendships and family support. Some adolescents who identify as gay or lesbian make their first suicide attempt within the year of "coming out" to themselves.[6] Religious conservatives, however, have challenged the major studies on suicide by homosexual adolescents.

Q81   What causes an individual to take her life?

"Suicide is a permanent solution to a temporary problem," noted Richard Seiden, who has studied suicides committed off the Golden Gate Bridge over a twenty-five year period.[1]

Eve Meyer, of the San Francisco Suicide Prevention Center, addresses the reality:

> Millions of people are walking around in a tremendous amount of pain, and our culture treats pain the way it treats underarm odor. We avoid it. We avoid the people who have it. . . . We're often surprised that these people chose death as a form of anesthesia. Most people who commit suicide do not want to die. But they have found the pain intolerable.[2]

Earl Grollman and Max Malikow say that a suicide leads us to wonder how well we knew the individual. "You see your friend as someone who had everything to live for. Her suicide shows that she believed she had something to die for. You might not ever know what that something was."[3] Furthermore, grief can be compounded by endless speculation, often by a police investigation that feels intrusive.

Certainly, depression is a significant factor in suicide, particularly if coupled with alcohol or substance abuse. Suicide also happens when an individual is thrust into a situation perceived to be chaotic or intolerable. Consider adolescents who find themselves rejected by a former friend or romantic interest and die by suicide, or the highly skilled individual who is terminated from meaningful employment and cannot find work. Admiral Tom Broda, a top naval official, committed suicide in 1996 amid media speculation that he had not earned the right to wear certain Vietnam War decorations. In a final note addressed "to my sailors," he wrote, "I couldn't bear to bring dishonor to you."[4]

Distorted thinking often leads to despair.

Some individuals perceive their lives, their community, or their family as futureless and undesirable. Corr, Nabe, and Corr suggest that three key elements influence the decision to attempt suicide: haplessness (being ill-fated or unlucky), helplessness (no one can help me now), and hopelessness. Sometimes, an experience or incident becomes "the last straw" that triggers a suicide attempt.[5]

These days we are also aware of the suicides motivated by political philosophies in some of the world's hot spots. "Suicide bombers" particularly in Israel and Iraq, believe they are undertaking this action in behalf of "their people" and their religion. Some believe they will become holy martyrs and receive great reward in heaven. Others find political conditions so intolerable they commit suicide in order to draw attention to them.

Q82   Why is suicide on the rise among the elderly?

The Centers for Disease Control reports suicide rates increase with age and are the highest among Americans sixty-five years and older. Males account for 84 percent of the suicides among the elderly. Suicide rates are the highest among the divorced or widowed elderly who have inadequate family support.[1] Some gerontologists think the elder rate is overlooked with the fixation on youth statistics.

Ill health, inadequate pain management, declining finances, or the acute fear of losing independence seem to be factors in many suicides among elders. Dick Gilbert, director of the World Pastoral Care Center, identifies two dominant factors as loneliness and the fear "of becoming a burden."[2] Other individuals have lost the will to live or want to be reunited with a deceased "loved one"—particularly after a long or intense marriage. What is particularly disturbing is the approximate twenty-five hundred murder/suicides—when a person "kills" a spouse or partner, then commits suicide. Some elderly make a pact to end their lives and marriages simultaneously.[3]

Some researchers expect suicide rates among the elderly to increase as baby boomers reach old age in an ageist culture. Contrary to the myth of the "golden years of retirement," many (particularly single) adults will experience economically challenging retirements with skyrocketing costs for medical care and an inadequate support system. According to Nancy Osgood of the Medical College of Virginia, even if the percentages of suicide among the elderly remain the same, the numbers of suicides will increase because of the number of aging baby boomers.[4]

Q83 What are some warning signs for a potential suicide?

Individuals indicate their suicidal intent in a variety of ways. Glen Evans and Norman Farberow identify four primary expressions:

- ✺ Verbal direct: "I will kill myself if you divorce/expose me."
- ✺ Verbal indirect: "A life without love is a life without meaning."

- Behavioral direct: An AIDS patient hoarding pain pills
- Behavioral indirect: Drivers taking risks in traffic

Other anticipatory signs are:
- Giving away prized possessions
- Sudden and extreme changes in eating habits or sleep patterns
- Withdrawal from friends, family, colleagues
- Changes in school or work performance
- Personality changes (nervousness, anger outbursts, apathy about health or appearance)
- Use of drugs or alcohol

Authors Lynne DeSpelder and Albert Strickland add another warning sign to the list: "The recent suicide of a friend or relative, or a history of previous suicide attempts."[1]

Two myths influence suicide. The first is that individuals who talk about suicide won't kill themselves. In reality, few people attempt suicide without having communicated intentions to others as hints, direct threats, or self-destructive actions. The second myth is that behavioral improvement means the crisis has passed. Hardly. In fact, making and finalizing the decision to end life can be exhilarating and freeing.[2]

Every suicide threat should be taken seriously.

Take to heart counselor Victor Parachin's guidance: "If you suspect, even remotely, that the suicide risk is high, get professional help immediately! Make an appointment with a therapist. Take your child [or the individual] to a crisis intervention center. Admit him or her to a hospital."[3]

Q84 Are males or females more likely to commit suicide?

Males are more than four times more likely to die from suicide than females. Yet, females are more likely to attempt suicide.[1] Young female adolescents "demonstrate more suicidal gestures."[2]

Historically, the risk of suicide has been greatest among white males. But recently, the CDC notes a significant increase in completed suicide among young black males.[3]

Q85 Should you tell a child that a family member or friend has committed suicide?

Yes, and according to grief specialist Helen Fitzgerald, "as soon as possible." A child "needs to be told everything you fear she will hear from relatives, friends, and their parents" or from the media. Information coming from a trusted individual will be less threatening.[1]

Fitzgerald suggests that the younger child be held when told and be given permission to cry. The discloser also needs to give himself or herself permission to cry.

If the child asks, "Why did (the person's name) kill himself?" Fitzgerald suggests answering, "Sometimes we can't understand why individuals die the way they do." Some people "have an illness of the mind that causes them to kill themselves. They have it; you don't, I don't."[2] It is also important that the child be assured she did not cause the death.

Fitzgerald believes a child should be told how the suicide took place—without being specific. She cautions, "If too much is kept hidden, however, I worry about what your child will imagine. Sometimes their imaginings can be worse than the truth." Finally, Fitzgerald urges the parent to encourage the child to ask questions and to tell the parent if she overhears something that troubles or confuses her.[3]

It is important to remember that "little ears" can hear more than we imagine. Editing the truth can have long-term consequences. When his wife, Francis, committed suicide, actor Henry Fonda, in consultation with his mother-in-law, made a decision to tell his children, Jane and Peter, that their mother had had a heart attack. Prior to this, Peter had made a bargain with Jesus that nothing "bad" would happen to his mother. Peter recalled, "It was Friday, April 14; Jesus had failed me. Jesus had let me down. Jesus forgot my prayer about Mother. I was too young to know that little in life was fair. . . . I never asked Jesus for anything again." Only years later would Peter Fonda discover how his mother died and the deception of his father and grandmother. [4]

Children's grief specialist Linda Goldman suggests that facts be disclosed in direct but not graphic details. She suggests using an explanation that suicide is

> the act of killing yourself so that your body won't work anymore. People may do this when they feel there is no other way they can think of to solve their problems, [when] there is no other way they can think of to escape their pain, or they may feel at the moment that life is not worth living. People can get help.[5]

Ask children to name places an individual could get help. Goldman explains, "Somewhere kids sense that they are being lied to, and uncertainty and potential rage become an all-pervasive part of their life."[6]

Goldman offers these suggestions for disclosure:

- Consider the child's age and awareness in explaining cause of death.
- Tell good stories about the deceased: "Remember the time . . ."
- Dispel myths.
- Be honest with your own feelings: "I wish Mom could have appreciated how much we all loved her and that somehow this would work out."

- Give permission to come to you with questions or anxieties. Remember this child may hear details or versions of the suicide from other children.
- Consider the child's bargains.[7] Peter Fonda's spiritual development as a child and as an adult had been drastically shaped by his mother's death. Your child may have made a similar request or bargain with God.

Q86   Is bereavement following a suicide different than when death happens from other causes?

It often is. Albert Hsu, whose elderly father committed suicide, wrote, "If we go on living, we will do so as people who see the world very differently."[1] One cliché often heard by grievers is, "At least, he is out of his pain." Hsu cites Anne-Grace Scheinin's observation: "Suicide doesn't end pain. It only lays it on the broken shoulders of the survivors."[2]

Grief following suicide is different in many ways. First, suicide survivors have to deal with abandonment issues. It is natural to feel abandoned when we lose someone we have loved. But the person who commits suicide, according to Earl Grollman and Max Malikow, "abandons those who love him" by choice.[3]

Second, there is "stigma residue" that is not experienced in other deaths. While attitudes on suicide have become more compassionate, there are individuals who have difficulty acknowledging that their loved one "completed the act of suicide." Initially, following a suicide, some individuals discover that old attitudes on suicide are "rebooted" and menace their thoughts. Attitudes on suicide, although diminished, have not disappeared.

Third, many survivors feel guilty for not having "read" the signs or for not having done more to prevent the suicide. Some feel guilty that their relationship was inadequate or failed to meet the needs of the one who committed suicide. This guilt complicates the bereaving.

Nancy Reuben Greenfield captured reality for some when she said, "Survivors ask 'Why?' long after the question has become unanswerable."[4] Commonly survivors protest, "But she had everything to live for," or "He is the last person I would have dreamed would have committed suicide." Indeed, some people will not accept suicide as an explanation, and that can be significantly divisive and create enormous tension between family members.

John Jordan, after serious study of the bereavement of suicide survivors, concludes the survivors feel more responsibility for the death, have more difficulty in making meaning or sense of the death, and have more feelings of anger toward the deceased for "perceived abandonment." Furthermore, "survivors expect that others will judge them more negatively, and thus may avoid seeking or accepting the social support that normally follows a death."[5] Some may collude with other family members to deny that a death was suicide or to keep it from public knowledge. "Compared to other forms of mourning," Jordan writes, "suicide survivors typically expend much more psychological energy trying to comprehend" the suicide.[6]

Albert Hsu expressed the anxieties of many conservative evangelical Christians over suicide:

> I have stopped worrying about my father's eternal fate. It does me no good to wonder about things that are impossible to know. . . . While I am hopeful that I will see my father again someday, I cannot cling to a false hope and claim with certainty that he is in heaven. That is not for me to say.[7]

I would respond it is also not for anyone to say that Mr. Hsu is *not* in heaven. It is important to be intensely supportive of suicide survivors who need, in Erica Goode's words, "a particular kind of tenderness."[8]

Q87 Does an individual who commits suicide go to hell?

For a considerable period of history, Christians believed that individuals who committed suicide died in mortal sin because they died without an opportunity to confess their sins. Moreover, the commandment, "Thou shall not kill," surely prohibited suicide. Among Catholics, those who carried out suicide could not receive a Requiem Mass or be buried in consecrated soil.

Given the growth of our understanding and the unfathomable love of God for humankind, few individuals believe that today. Yet, in times of stress, such as a suicide, individuals may resort back to old theological ideas. Dietrich Bonhoeffer wrote, "Who would venture to say that God's grace and mercy cannot embrace and sustain even a man's failure to resist this hardest of all temptations."[1]

Gilbert Meilaender also offers helpful insight:

Contrary to what Christians have often believed, . . . suicide does not necessarily damn one. The [person who commits] suicide dies, so to speak, in the moment of sinning, without opportunity to repent. But then, so may I be killed instantly in a car accident while plotting revenge against an enemy of mine. God judges persons, not individual deeds, and the moment in one's life when a sinful deed occurs does not determine one's fate.[2]

15. Questions about the Death of a Pet

"My life changed irrevocably. Rocky's loss taught me how deeply we grieve for our loved animals, the intensity of pain, the length of time it can last, and how one's life can be forever changed. . . . I learned firsthand that grief for a companion animal matters, even though we live in a world that reminds us repeatedly that grief for an animal doesn't count as much as grief for a person. The anniversary of his death taught me the reality of anniversary grief."
—*Betty J. Carmack*[1]

"If heaven can be happier for us with animals, then you can be sure God will supply them for us."
—*Billy Graham*[2]

Q88 I have a friend whose dog died. You would think a family member died. How can I tactfully remind him, "It was only a dog, for heaven's sake."

For many individuals the death of a pet is experienced as a disenfranchised loss. Owners of animals would rarely agree, "It was only a dog." Many individuals, even professionals, may not appreciate the emotional suffering a beloved pet's death can have on an individual and on a family.

Some individuals bond with animals in a way they do not bond with humans. One visitor to the White House was surprised to find a bird perched on Thomas Jefferson's shoulder. The president noticed the person's surprise and explained, "Do not be disturbed by Curious. I needed something to love, and when I found a little mockingbird, I tamed it and it became my friend."[1]

You did not mention the age of the individual or the age of his dog, but watching a pet age and become a fraction of what the pet had once been, is a difficult anticipatory grief. The decision to euthanize a beloved pet is very difficult. How one makes the decision—and whether it is for the owner's or for the pet's benefit—can make a difference in the grieving process.

All individuals need permission to grieve for their pets. In her book *Grieving the Death of a Pet*, pet loss specialist Betty Carmack points out that animals offer a constancy and stability which are essential in a companion's life. "Their animals had been their one stable and constant presence. To lose this reassuring equilibrium and balance is to be painfully shaken at the core of one's being."[2]

In November 1992, President George H. W. Bush lost his reelection bid. Two weeks later his mother died. Then in the spring of 1993, his favorite dog, Ranger, died. Barbara Bush observed, "I think he let Ranger be sort of the tunnel of mourning. You can't cry, if you're a man, over an election. You can't cry over your mother, I guess." But Ranger's death devastated Bush.[3]

Q89   Will our pets be in heaven?

Betty Carmack responds, "For many, reconstructing their world means holding onto the belief that they'll be reunited with their beloved animal companion. Looking forward to being together again is a hope that gives meaning to life."[1] She quotes one pet companion, "I can't help but believe that if God is love, he wouldn't abandon any of his loving creatures, and pets are certainly that. Hopefully, he has a special place for them in heaven, and one day I will experience this unconditional love again."[2]

I am sure some individuals did a double take when Billy Graham, in his syndicated newspaper column, tackled the issue. Quick to insist that only humans have souls, he went on to say, "I firmly believe that if animals are needed to make our happiness there complete, then God will provide them! God knows our needs, and one of the joys of heaven is that all our needs will be fully met."[3]

Q90 How can I show compassion to a friend whose pet died?

Start by saying simply, "I am sorry your pet died." (It will be helpful if you call the pet by name.) Second, send a card expressing your condolence. Third, ask the grieving pet owner to tell you a favorite story about the pet. Or ask how they plan to memorialize their pet. And finally, pray for the grieving individual. You will pray more intelligently, if you ask your friend, from time to

For some children, the death of a pet is the first introduction to significant loss.

time, how she/he is doing. Supporting your friend in these ways gives him or her permission to mourn the loss of a loved pet in a culture that may hint, "It was only a dog (or cat or bird or snake . . .)!"

16. Questions about Grief and Sexuality

"Sex may be a positive way of communicating, to express love, support, comfort, and tenderness for each other."
—*Rana K. Limbo and Sara Rich Wheeler*[1]

"Adult children of older people often find it difficult to deal with the sexuality of their parents because they are influenced by the common stereotype that older adults are asexual. In addition, children of older adults who are widowed may discourage intimate relationships because of concern about their inheritance."
—*Carol Miller*[2]

Q91 How soon after a child's death should a couple resume sexual relations?

This depends upon the couple. Some couples are anxious about initiating sex because it can be a reminder of how the child was conceived. Some may fear being rebuffed for initiating sexual intimacy. In too many instances, one partner has reacted angrily, "Is that all you can think of?"

Unfortunately, the topic of sexual interest is almost taboo. Some couples cannot talk openly about sexuality. In some cases, couples are so deep in their individual grief they cannot accommodate the grief of a spouse or partner. Partners may be insensitive to each other's particular grief style and out of tune with their needs. It is no surprise that sexual interest at this time can be miscommunicated and misinterpreted.

The Bible discloses the sexual comforting of David and Bathsheba after the death of their unnamed son. "Then David comforted his wife Bathsheba, and he went to her and lay with her" (2 Samuel 12:24). Some grieving spouses, male as well as female, want lots of touch, holding, and comforting before they want sexual intercourse.

For some individuals, the sexual coupling is a reminder of their togetherness in facing this loss. Rana Limbo and Sara Rich Wheeler, specialists in perinatal loss, have addressed this topic:

> When a couple loses a baby, they are affected in so many ways. The same intimacy that created their child may be difficult now. Or, they may find it a source of great strength. Whatever a couple's relationship was before the baby was born, it more than likely will be different afterwards.[1]

For other partners, sex can be an escape. As one couple told Limbo and Wheeler, "Sometimes [sex] was the one thing we could count on. It was a few minutes when we could shut ourselves off and stop thinking about how bad we felt."[2]

Dr. Rebekah Wang-Cheng comments that most grievers "know from experience that sex is a great stress reliever. Sexual orgasm releases endorphins in the brain—chemical substances that relieve pain and result in a 'runner's high'"[3] or perhaps in this case, "a griever's high." The danger comes in using sex to dodge unwanted feelings and thoughts. Some grievers may feel a sense of shame or guilt for having "used" a partner to escape the grief momentarily.

One of the most important elements for surviving for grieving parents is communication skills. It may be quite different to initiate a conversation about sexual intimacy; for some couples, such a conversation is difficult even in normal times. Try these conversation starters:

- ❧ "This may be difficult for you to hear, but I need to tell you that I am struggling sexually."
- ❧ "I want to be close to you. I would like . . ."
- ❧ "I have always valued our intimacy. What level of sexual intimacy would you feel comfortable with right now?"

Couples do need to talk. How that conversation is initiated may determine the productivity of the conversation.

Q92 Our five-year-old died three months ago. My husband (and his mother) wants us to have another child immediately. Should we?

It is impossible to "replace" a child. Each child is a distinct, one-of-a-kind gift of God, a unique personality. At one time, physicians and members of the family were quick to urge a couple to have a child right away. Even if the word "replace" was not used, the idea was communicated. Some people also viewed pregnancy as a distraction from the grief.

Anything, including a pregnancy, that distracts from grief complicates your situation and prevents you from doing thorough grief work.

Q93 Sometimes I think the only way my husband can be tender is to have sex. I am not ready for intercourse. How can I tell him I just want to be held and touched?

Many men do not know how to be intimate without involving sex. They have not been conditioned to be vulnerable or tender. In addition, men are socialized to hide or control their grief. After the death of his first-born, Martin Luther wrote, "My soul is almost like a woman's, so moved am I with misery, I could never have believed that the hearts of parents are so tender toward their children."[1] Lovemaking, or sexmaking, sometimes offers men a chance to lay aside the armor and be human.

If you, however, are not ready, you need to convey that to your partner. Leslie Schover, who works with cancer patients on sexuality issues, offers this advice: "Let your partner know that you will want to have sex as soon as you feel better. Give your partner some ideas on helping you feel more sexual again, such as, 'Try being affectionate in a relaxed way' or 'Let me know you still find me attractive.'"[2]

Sexual orgasm offers some relief from sadness because of the release of brain chemicals like endorphins and phenylethylamine, PEA, into the bloodstream during orgasm. The sexual intimacy is, for some, a welcome break from the all-encompassing reality of grief.

Grief is tough and demanding. Some people look for a "fix" to lift them out of the darkness or sadness.

Talk to your spouse about your sexual needs and about how you perceive your partner's sexual and intimacy needs. If you do not want intercourse yet, say so. Make certain your partner hears that you are rejecting intercourse and not your partner. Truth be told, your spouse may be equally unready. Find ways you can honor the needs of your spouse.

For most couples, sex feels good. Unfortunately, some get the idea they are betraying the person who died by feeling good. Interestingly, in Judaism, sexual relations are forbidden during the seven-day *shiva* period, as is shaving, bathing, having a haircut, and other everyday acts. That "prohibition" can take the pressure off in early grief adjustment.

Q94 I do not want to initiate sex with my wife because she is taking our son's death so hard. I am conflicted over this. Is masturbation wrong for me?

Life has a way of re-introducing us to issues we thought were long ago jettisoned. Masturbation is normal. Masturbation is normal among grievers. It is what we tell ourselves about the practice that complicates it. Too many adults think of masturbation as some kind of second-rate, "junior varsity" sexual experience. But masturbation during grief is a way of getting in touch with our bodies. For those who may be hesitant to initiate sex with a spouse, or whose partners have made it clear they are not ready for sex, masturbation can be a harmless alternative.

Unfortunately, too many adults cannot talk about their sexual needs, desires, and longings. Sometimes, the "balance of sexual power" in a marriage shifts following a death; sometimes grief forever changes the sexual dynamic. Many spouses have groaned, "I just want things back like they were. But my wife is so sad all the time. It's a downer!" In reality, you may not get back to a sexual "normal." But you may, with patience, create a new sexual normal.

Q95 My wife and I had a great sex life. Now, after her death, I am fighting a real battle over my sex drive. What can I do?

I am glad you experienced a "great sex life." Not every widower has that memory. In fact, some widowers rehearse the fact that they had a poor sex life and tell themselves it's time to make up for lost time in new sexual relationship(s). Yet, other grieving spouses are afraid they will not have as good a sexual relationship as they had.

I would not consider sexual memories to be fantasies. Be glad you have these. Believe that, in your future, there might be new good sexual memories, if you don't say yes to every sexual invitation that comes along.

Dr. Rebekah Wang-Cheng addressed this issue in a letter on HealthLink, sponsored by the University of Wisconsin. Masturbation "probably never can be as fulfilling and satisfying as sex between two people who love each other, but when you're widowed, you don't have many options." She adds, "Sex is a God-given gift for our well being [Dr. Wang-Cheng's theological opinion] and is not a sin when not abused and in the right context."[1]

Q96 My father is older and recently widowed. While at his house cleaning out some of my mother's things in the medicine cabinet, I found a prescription for Viagra. Why does he need Viagra?

Lots of grieving men use Viagra. Although you may be unable to imagine your grieving father as a sexual person, he is. Grief can have an effect on the libido and on sexual performance. Your father, regardless of his age, may be exploring his sexuality as a means of coping with his grief or of seeking a future. Hopefully, this medication is physician-prescribed rather than purchased over the Internet, because there could be potential medical complications.

Q97 My mother died six months ago and my father is already dating! (And I think he is doing more than dating.) He is acting like a sixteen-year-old! What should I say to him?

So, now you are the parent waiting up, wondering what is going on? In the death of a parent, we sometimes switch responsibilities.

You did not mention the age of your father or any factors in your mother's death. Sometimes, during a long illness, a forced celibacy prevails. Thus, it may have been some time since your father has had sexual relations. What is he is telling himself about that? Whose voices is he listening to?

Dating may not be such a bad thing. Admittedly, too many men who have lost their partners jump into serious romantic relationships because they are lonely. But many widowers simply want someone to talk to, eat with, etc. This may be what your father is seeking. Of course there are widowers who have sabotaged their grief by a premature remarriage (and subsequent divorce). It also needs to be said that there are opportunists out there, especially if your father has money, a home, can drive, can dance, etc., who will take advantage of his grief.

Many widowers simply want companionship.

Some older males seek solace in sexual intimacy even if it is transitional or casual. Some males, after the death of a spouse, use prostitutes or escort services. Some look to cyberintimacy on the Internet. They may reason, "Well, no one gets hurt this way."

It is difficult to realize that roles change between parents and adult children. If the son or daughter can spend some time asking: "What troubles me about this?" and then can lovingly communicate that concern, all parties will be able to deal with the concerns more objectively. These are, by their very nature, very difficult conversations. Two suggestions:

- ❧ Try to imagine your father's perspective. At his age, what is it like to be alone? Maybe he thinks you are too busy for him. Maybe he does not want to be a burden on you. Maybe your mother's illness has heightened his fear of illness. Given the reality that so many women outlive men, some males are looking for another caretaker. Consider what his reasons for dating are.

~ Examine *your* responses. Do you feel his dating—and whatever—is dishonoring your mother's memory? Many adult children have expressed the thought, "Mom's not even cold in the ground!" Would you feel differently about your father dating in three months? Six months? A year? Some adult children take the approach, "I just want him to be happy." Others respond, "I don't care what he does as long as he does not *marry* her." What may go unsaid is "and compromise the ultimate distribution of assets." What exactly are your concerns?

If you do have concerns you want to share with your father, rehearse what you want to say. Conversations with parents about dating can go badly because of the role reversal. In the heat of the moment, ugly things can be said that will be hard to forget or forgive. Admittedly, the conversation is awkward. It may have been years since your father has thought about STDs and the risks of unprotected sex.

Consider how best to approach him (or how someone else should approach him). This may be influenced by the nature of your relationship before the death. Take into account the risk of alienating your father. Expect some siblings to be uncomfortable speculating on a father's sex life. Anticipate disagreement and responses such as "Mind your own business!"

Q98 I have discovered that my husband has been surfing porn sites on the Internet. He keeps promising me it will not happen again, but it does. Could our daughter's death have anything to do with this?

Of course. Your husband may feel like someone has altered his life script without his permission. He may feel powerless. The grief may be chafing his sense of control. He may be afraid to initiate sex with you. The Internet offers abundant opportunities for sexual interest and gratification (for a fee). And he does not have to disclose the grief in creating a cyberidentity. Some men carry such a paralyzing load of grief that they are willing to do anything to be distracted, even for a few minutes, and even if it results in discovery.

Some men perceive cyberporn as the lesser of two or three evils. In their thinking, no one is being hurt. In fact, they may justify it as a way of not upsetting you. Grief forces men to re-examine their sense of power. If they feel powerless in preventing the death, those questions may transfer into their sexual prowess.

Cyberporn offers an illusive sense of power and sexual attraction. Cyberporn is destructive and manipulative. You are right to be concerned about this choice by your husband because it is, in essence, a way of numbing himself against the pain following your daughter's death. Approach him gently with your awareness.

Q99 Since his mother's death, my sixteen-year-old son has been having sex with his girlfriend. I do not approve. What is going on?

Many adolescents do not know how to "handle" grief feelings and the first acquaintance with vulnerability. Grief makes them significantly different than their peers and makes conversation awkward. Many adolescent males do not know how to experience tenderness other than physically. Your son actually may not intend to have intercourse, but he may want to be held, touched, and comforted—and that desire evolves into intercourse. There are lots of risks when intercourse is not anticipated but happens, a sexually transmitted disease and pregnancy being two immediate concerns.

Talk to your son even though it may be difficult to initiate the conversation. If you do not, you could be dealing with a whole new dynamic in nine months, not to mention risking your son's health.

Q100 My forty-one-year-old husband was killed in a car wreck six weeks ago. I thought we had a good marriage. Like many couples, we had our ups and downs. Because our sex life had been dull, I suspected another woman. While cleaning out his home office, I found gay porn magazines and videos. Was my husband gay?

Certain realities come to awareness after a death. For some it is the presence of another person in a loved one's life. In this case, you apparently have not found evidence of a person, but of a sexual experience or experimentation.

Do not jump to any conclusions. Some individuals would find the evidence "proof," but sexual orientation is much more complex. Certainly, numbers of married men are gay, homosexual, bisexual, or, in the new description, MSM, "males who have sex with males." Many males who have sex with men would never identify themselves as gay, homosexual, or bisexual. Some knew of the same-sex attraction before they married; others began exploring that orientation after marriage.

This "secret" may have been an enormous emotional strain on your husband. He was not exploring this or experiencing this to hurt you. In fact, he may have been working overtime to hide this from you so that you would not be hurt. Some married men believe it is just a phase.

Sexual secrets are an element in many marital landscapes. Give it some time for serious reflection before you come to any conclusions. Explore this issue with a counselor who is knowledgeable about married homosexuals or bisexuals.

Q101 I feel guilty. I was never interested in sex with my husband while he was alive. Quite frankly, he did not take care of himself physically and his idea of sex was pretty boring. Now, as a widow, I have begun dating and am finding that I am interested in sex. What should I do with these feelings?

- Acknowledge them. I suggest a journal as a starting point.
- Discuss these feelings with a counselor or therapist. Sometimes guilt can be a co-companion to grief. You may have a sense of regret about the image of marriage you portrayed. Some individuals may have assumed you had a "wonderful" relationship. Many individuals have a public marital persona that does not match private reality. (Ask their children!) Some grieve a relationship that "was not" rather than a relationship that was.
- Be cautious. In widowhood, some individuals believe you need to be "sexually serviced." These sexual opportunists can "read" you and suggest, sometimes rather crassly, "I know what you need, *if you know what I mean*." Some widows have been stunned by how direct men have been about their sexual needs (and, in this era of equal opportunity, some widowers have been stunned by the directness of females).
- Guard. Guard your heart. Guard your body. Guard your bank account and investments. You are not sixteen, but you may find yourself wooed and literally "swept off your feet." Do not think this is a "last chance" for romance.
- Take it to the Lord in prayer. Use Martin Luther's words after the death of his daughter that he wrote to a friend, "Pray the Lord for me!"[1]

Q102 I am seventy-five years old. My daughter
recently told me she is disgusted with me.
A man "my age," according to her, should
not even have a sex drive. She says I "am
embarrassing her and the whole family."
What do I say to her?

Ask her to pronounce two words: father and adult. Our capacity for
sexual expression and experience does not end with any particular
birthday. Nor does it end with the death of a spouse or partner. This
may be more about her issues of aging and anxieties than yours.

I counseled an older widower whose physician son berated
him for acting like a "damned sixteen-year-old." Living in a
small community, the son contended that "everyone is talking
about you!" The father, sheepishly, asked me, "I am not too old,
am I?" He did not want to hurt his son or himself.

I suggested he tell his son that he is proud of raising a doctor and a wise one at that. Yet he is stunned to find out his son
cut classes in medical school—because he must have been
absent the days they talked about senior adults and sexuality.

"Oh, Dr. Smith," the widower laughed, "I couldn't do that."

"Sure you can," I replied. "Because if your son is prejudicial
toward your sexual concerns, he is prejudiced toward some of
his older patients."

Think through the concerns your daughter could have. Does
she feel you are dating too soon? Too much? Too openly? Or that
you're dating the wrong person? Talk to her about it. One ugly
reality is that some adult children use sexual fear to disguise
their bottom-line fear: You will meet someone, remarry, and
there goes a significant portion of the inheritance. The motives
of some adult children are not always pure.

17. Questions about Funeral Rituals and Customs

"Funerals press the noses of the faithful against
the windows of their faith."
—*Thomas Lynch*[1]

"We do not get all our ritual needs met in one stop or one
cemetery. There is a need to re-ritualize down the road.
That can be as simple as lighting a candle on a birthday
or taking flowers to the cemetery on the anniversary
of the death."
—*Harold Ivan Smith*[2]

"I am convinced, more than ever, that our culture has
labeled as 'weird' some of the most wonderful, precious
and sensitive acts of grieving and love imaginable. . . .
Our culture's labels of what is weird and what is
appropriate about grieving are hurtful and harmful.
We may choose to keep our secrets but we need not feel
strange about choosing our own path for grieving."
—*Barbara K. Roberts*[3]

Q103 Why do we need a wake or visitation?

Historically, the wake was needed in the days before embalming to provide individuals to sit with the body to see if there was any chance of life and to give families an opportunity to rest. George Washington ordered in his will, "Have me decently buried and do not let my body be put in the vault in less than three days after I am dead."[1] No one wanted to be buried prematurely before embalming became common.

As medical and embalming practices advanced, the need to ensure the deceased was indeed dead diminished. But the practice of holding a wake endured to provide loved ones with a venue to "pay their last respects."

Long ago, visitations were held in the family's residence, but this imposed on their privacy. The development of the funeral home changed this practice. Holding a wake at a funeral home also protects the residence from unknown individuals coming, staying, and taxing the resources of the family.

Individuals bring three gifts to a visitation:

- The gift of sympathy expressed in simple words: "I am so sorry."
- The gift of promises of assistance or future assistance: "Is there anything I can do?" or "If you need me, just call."
- The gift of stories and assessments of the life of the deceased: "I will always remember the time . . ." Some people while living are reticent to draw attention to themselves, so they share only portions of their life stories. At a visitation, survivors often learn more details about their loved one's life.

I often describe wakes using the Hawaiian word *humuhumu*, which means "to fit the pieces together." Friends, neighbors, and coworkers come to visitations bearing memory fragments, which we fit or weave together. The visitation also reminds of the width, breadth, and depth of our relational networks.

Q104 Why have a funeral?

Thirty years ago that would have been an outrageous question. Today it is "the" question for some families and individuals. In a hurry-up, get-on-with-life culture, funerals and a corpse are a big inconvenience. Yet funerals serve a much larger purpose than allowing mourners to witness the final disposition of the body or the cremated remains. Therese Rando, one of the leading thanatologists in the country, identifies both psychological and sociological benefits for a funeral. Funerals:

- ◦ confirm and reinforce the reality of the death;
- ◦ assist in the acknowledgment and expression of feelings of loss;
- ◦ offer the survivors a vehicle for addressing their feelings;
- ◦ stimulate recollection about the deceased;
- ◦ assist mourners in beginning to accommodate the changed relationship between themselves and the deceased's loved one;
- ◦ allow for input from the community, which serves as a living memorial to the deceased and helps mourners form an integrated image of the deceased.[1]

The social functions of funerals are important because they remind us "no one is an island," in the words of English theologian John Donne. The death of an individual touches a lot of shoreline in the emotional lives of a community. Doug Manning asks, "Can you imagine the impact on our nation if President [John F.] Kennedy had been immediately cremated and his body buried in secrecy? Or can you imagine England not having a state funeral when Princess Diana died?"[2] In this sense, funerals:

- ◦ allow the community to provide social support to the mourners;
- ◦ provide meaningful, structured activities to counter the loss of predictability and order frequently accompanying the death of a loved one;

~o~ begin the process of reintegrating the bereaved back into the community.[3]

Christian funerals are dual-focused: We honor the life of the deceased *and* we celebrate the resurrection of Jesus. Countless grievers have found comfort in Jesus's promise-packed words,

> "Do not let your hearts be troubled. Trust in God; trust also in me. In my Father's house are many rooms; if it were not so, I would have told you. I am going to prepare a place for you. And if I go and prepare a place for you, I will come back and take you to be with me that you also may be where I am" (John 14:1-3).

Through music, scripture, story, poetry, and touch, funerals allow grievers to express the coherence of our faith. The community reaffirms its beliefs, priorities, and values. Admittedly, funerals can painfully remind us that we, as well as family members and friends, will die. Yet they also call to mind our significant hope in joining the eternal community of faith.

Above all, funerals provide comfort for the family and community alike. They stimulate the collective memories of the grievers and help re-cement social coherence. Some memories would never link up other than in the funeral envi-

Funerals are ways a community says: "Your loved one's life counted. You are not going to be left alone to get through this. And, most important, your loved one will be remembered!"

ronment. Often, through a funeral experience, we hear in another's words the words we had been seeking, and words that become, in time, comfort to us. Funerals "rub our faces" in the reality of death but also remind us we need not go through the experience of mourning alone.

Q105 Is it possible to have a funeral after the loved one is buried?

Technically, no. A funeral is a service with a corpse present; a memorial service is a ritual without the corpse. However, it is never too late to create a ritual of grief and remembrance. You will need to find a cooperative minister or celebrant (one who conducts funerals/memorial services).

Q106 Isn't a funeral with a body present archaic?

Thomas Lynch, a funeral director, would ask, "Have you attended a wedding where the bride was absent? Have you attended a baby baptism where the baby was absent? Have you attended an ordination where the ordinand is absent? Their presence is essential to the ritual. Yet, in a death-denying society, ritual planners want to avoid having to deal with a corpse."[1]

You may not like all the traditional features of a funeral, such as having an open casket or expecting friends and neighbors to view the corpse and offer comment. It seems wiser to adapt or modify the funeral than to dispense with it.

Q107 Should the committal be just for family?

Historically, the committal was part of a three interlocking rituals open to all mourners: the viewing, the funeral, and the committal. In fact, long ago one of the assessments of a person's standing in the community was the length of the funeral procession to the cemetery. Today, especially in urban areas with traffic congestion, there is a growing movement to discourage the funeral procession. Even with police escorts, the procession becomes difficult for the mourners and community alike. Sometimes the realism of traffic patterns between a funeral home or church and a particular cemetery can influence who is invited to the cemetery.

The cemetery can be too much reality for some individuals.

At some point, cemeterians started to soften "reality" by using artificial grass to hide the dirt pile that would eventually

cover the casket. In some cases, even the hole was lined to hide the dirt. Over the years, the committal service has also been shortened. It used to be that mourners stayed for the lowering of the casket into the grave. In Jewish ceremonies, it is traditional that family members shovel dirt onto the casket. I concede that that sound can be a stark reminder of the finality of death.

Increasingly, some families prefer to hold a private burial for emotional reasons. At the visitation and funeral, family members sometimes feel as if they are "on duty," needing to be strong or "hold up well" in front of certain individuals. The private burial gives the family a chance—beyond prying eyes—to freely express their emotions.

Rituals invite us to pay close attention to the passings and the pivotal moments in life. As a traditionalist who believes in going to the grave, I often quote the advice of Michigan funeral director, Thomas Lynch: "Go to the hole in the ground. Stand over it. Look into it. Wonder. And be cold. But stay until it's over. Until it is done."[1]

Q108 I often wish we had had a memorial service rather than a funeral for my son. I went through the funeral on automatic pilot. What else can we do to memorialize our son?

Because of the seventy-two-hour time period for holding rituals with an embalmed body, many grievers are physically present yet emotionally absent during funerals. Thus, they miss the comfort rituals provide. Some funeral directors recommend audiotaping or videotaping services, particularly when the death was unexpected or traumatic.

Too many people believe the funeral or memorial service brings to a close the public mourning. In fact, it is only the end of the *beginning* phase. There are opportunities for additional rituals at important moments. I have loved the Jewish rituals of *yitzhreit*, which honors the anniversary of a death, and *yitzor*, which is a prayer that acknowledges the death on the Jewish Holy days. In Judaism, special attention is also given to the unveiling of the tombstone or marker on the one-year mark.

Some grievers join fun runs and walks to raise money to fight the disease that took their loved ones. Some people participate in memorial rituals at Advent, Christmas, Mother's or Father's Day, or Valentine's Day. They may buy a plant for a flower garden or make a donation to a cause. Such rituals communicate that this day on the calendar has been altered by the death of someone special to them.

Rituals do not have to be highly organized in order to be meaningful. Family members may value the intentional lighting of a candle or a moment of silence or sharing memories on birthdays, anniversaries, or at holiday gatherings. They may visit a tree planted in the person's memory, sing a favorite hymn, or look through a photo album. There are many creative ways to honor and remember a loved one's passing long after the funeral.

Q109 My husband is something of a stickler for always "doing the right thing." He thinks we ought to "hang out" at a visitation. I think we should drop in, pay our respects, and move on. Which one of us is right?

Visitations or wakes trouble many adults because they require direct confrontation with the reality of death, and, often, its unpredictability. Imagine for a moment you are the griever, whether a widow or the father of a deceased daughter. Would you want friends and neighbors to "drop in, pay respects, and move on" or would you want them to hang around?

I concede that Emily Post thinks "dropping in" is acceptable. In a time-conscious society such as ours, an expectation that friends will spend considerable time at a visitation may be unrealistic. Post validates brevity: "The visit to the funeral home need not last more than five or ten minutes. As soon as the visitor has expressed his sympathy to each member of the family, and spoken a moment or two with those he knows well, he may leave."[1] To me, that sounds too much like, "Express it and beat it!"

Today, everyone is busy. We have settled for one night of visitation, or even just one hour preceding the service. As a traditionalist, however, I remember the custom of holding multiple nights, or days, of visitation. Friends attended many times. Individuals talked, caught up with old friends, and sometimes made new friends. After all, what is the root word of visitation? *Visit.*

Q110 How well do you need to know someone to attend the visitation or funeral?

These days, too many individuals wonder: Do I know the deceased or family members well enough to be inconvenienced? Visitations introduce some family members to the deceased's social orbit. Individuals come paying respects and bringing snippets of stories that help grievers understand a loved one influenced more lives than imagined. Your "I'm sorry" is woven into a quilt of condolences that bring comfort to the family of the deceased. Go!

Q111 Why is there such sad music at funerals? I want something spirited when I am buried. How do I make sure my musical preferences will be honored?

Historically, individuals have sung their faith, especially when they didn't know what to say. David Cole says, "It is in singing hymns, psalms, choruses, and liturgical text that worshipers vocalize their faith." Moreover, hymns "enable us to make connections with important learnings and to reinforce our understandings."[1] Martin Rinkert, at the end of the Thirty Years War, wrote the hymn, "Now Thank We All Our God." Rinkert had conducted as many as five thousand funerals (sometimes fifty a day during the war and plague).

Originally, funerals were worship services, and the belief in resurrection was reflected musically. However, the trend toward using popular music has been building for about fifteen years, as more baby boomers plan funerals or memorial services or die themselves. Dave Tianen says the days of the funeral organ are over and funeral music may include "every stripe of popular music, including rock, country, swing and polka." Elton John's reworked "Candle in the Wind" for Princess Diana's funeral has sold some thirty-three million copies. Funeral directors report Eric Clapton's "Tears in Heaven," Frank Sinatra's "My Way," and Bette Middler's "Wind Beneath My Wings" are frequent requests.[2] Mark Krause, a funeral director in Milwaukee, laughs, "Frank Sinatra gets played here more than in Las Vegas." *The Director*, the official magazine of the National Funeral Directors Association, identifies other popular funeral or memorial service music as Bob Dylan's "Knocking on Heaven's Door," The Police's "Every Breath You Take," Led Zeppelin's "Stairway to Heaven," Elvis Presley's "Always on My Mind," and Terry Jack's "Seasons in the Sun."[3] "Amazing Grace," in various styles, also remains popular.

There is concern among church leaders that the music has become too personal and can be offensive. The Catholic Diocese of Providence, Rhode Island, for example, has banned "Danny Boy." One friend finished a committal only to hear (on a boom box which a mourner had brought), "Great Balls of Fire."

If you want spirited music, make your wishes known to your family, preferably in writing.

Q112 I think flowers are a waste of money. My wife disagrees. I believe the family or a designated charity can use the money far more effectively. We both feel strongly about our positions. What guidance can you offer us?

Flowers historically disguised smells of decomposition in the days before embalming. Today, people use flowers to convey their sentiment. Gerald Euster found that flowers are a "strategic social action" for the elderly who may not be able to "get out" or come to a visitation or funeral. Because of the strong sense of social obligation many seniors have, it gives them a way of "paying respects."[1]

Flowers also are a way of jump-starting conversations. Most individuals are a little uneasy in a funeral home. So a simple statement like "Joan would have loved all these flowers" may gain an agreement *and* a "How did you know Joan?"

In a column in *The Kansas City Star*, Bill Tammeus addressed the question, "Why do we bring flowers to graves?" He concluded, "I think part of our motivation is fear. We are afraid that some day no one will remember—or even know—that we ever lived. We can foresee a day when our graves are ignored, forgotten a little more permanently each day until finally it will be as if we had never been here."[2]

I come from a family that did not send flowers. My father always said, "They can't eat flowers next week." So he gave cash to the family, especially to widows.

Two practical factors may also influence the decision not to send flowers. First, floral arrangements are expensive, particularly for a one-hour visitation. Second, some cemeteries restrict the number of floral displays they will accept. When my dad died, all the flowers had to be left outside the entrance to the mausoleum. So my mom and I took some and placed them on graves of friends of the family. You may wish to consider how the flowers will be enjoyed after the funeral.

Q113 Why are funerals getting shorter?

Many individuals believe short funerals benefit the bereaved. But I feel shorter services are one way the culture denies, or limits, grief. Spending time in the presence of a corpse challenges your sense of power and invincibility, especially when you may have played golf with the deceased the day before.

Too many funerals are generic by-the-book services that do not recognize the particularness of the deceased. Some families, especially where there is some level of dysfunction or estrangement from the deceased, or between family members, originate the directive: "Let's get this over with as quickly as possible."

Short, "just get it over" funerals leave individuals feeling liturgically or ritually diminished. This trend is not new. When President Warren G. Harding died in San Francisco on August 2, 1923, First Lady Florence Harding requested that the Reverend James West offer a "brief" prayer in the presidential suite. Later, she asked him to conduct a service "not to exceed fifteen minutes" before the presidential party left to return the president's corpse to the White House.[1] Moreover, the service at the Capitol was very brief. If a president's or celebrity's service is short, that sends a message to future funeral planners.

Some families, sensitive to the busy schedules of friends and associates, want to honor time constraints. In large, urban areas where commute times may be a factor, there are informal demands for short, or at least shorter, services. If there is to be a procession to a cemetery, given traffic flow in some communities, that can be an added factor.

When making funeral plans, you need to know the director's plans. In the culture of some funeral homes, they want to "turn over" the parlor, chapel, and facilities as quickly as possible for the next family or client. Some individuals feel rushed.

I have not forgotten a service for a university freshman who died in a dorm fire. The service ran long because so many individuals took Eucharist. I happened to be standing next to the funeral director when someone walked up and indignantly demanded, "How much longer is this going to go on?" Softly but firmly, the funeral director said, "It will go on as long as that family in the front row needs it to go on."

There are funerals or memorial services that "go on and on" because no one can think of a way to bring them to a close. Or perhaps no one wants to face the reality of a trip to a cemetery. Yet in some ethnic communities, services run longer because the underlying philosophy is, "We are going to do what it takes to have a funeral."

Q114 Do you have to be a minister to conduct a funeral?

No, although if a funeral takes place in a community of faith (a church, a temple, etc.), their requirements take precedent. Some readers will remember when a Roman Catholic had to obtain the permission of a priest to attend a Protestant funeral. Historically, one reason for the development of funeral home chapels was to reduce some of the "turf issues."

Some families do not want a minister, priest, or rabbi presiding because of conflict issues. Or they feel, "Well, he wasn't religious," or "She did not go to church." Some individuals have strong feelings on this topic because they have experienced a minister who emotionally manipulated the funeral service. Others have a bad impression from ministers who seemed to be as in a big hurry to "get it over with."

In a real sense, funeral and memorial services are for the living.

Victor Parachin reports that good funerals help individuals "make sense of what seems senseless."[1] The right minister, priest, or rabbi can be an incredible "gift" to the family, friends, and associates who gather for a service to honor the life of the deceased. Even if religion isn't a prominent practice in the family's life, many clergy are comfortable in creating what might be called a "faith-lite" service that is more representative of the wishes of the family.

For years, funeral directors have recommended "for hire" ministers to lead services for strangers. Unfortunately, these ministers have provided very little pastoral care to the grieving families.

Recently, Celebrants, a program popular in Australia, has been introduced in the United States. Celebrants are certified to conduct a secular (although the service may have religious elements) funeral or memorial service. Celebrants are trained to design unique, personalized services that reflect the interests of the deceased and the family. They work, not unlike wedding planners, to create a service that is dignified and meaningful.

Q115 What is the difference between a funeral director, a mortician, and an undertaker?

The profession of caring for the dead goes back thousands of years. Brent Russell identifies Joseph of Arimathaea as "the patron saint of funeral directors." "It may be significant," he writes, "that no apostle or any surviving family member approached civil authorities" with the request for Jesus's body. "If not for Joseph, there would have been no tomb from which Jesus would have resurrected" because criminals' bodies were "left to decompose in full view at the site of the execution."[1]

In the early period of Christian history, the Fossores were the gravediggers and sextons who cared for the dead. Todd Van Beck has described the rigors of their work:

By virtue of their obligation to care for the Christian dead, the Fossores were placed in an extremely difficult position. The danger historically emanated from the Caesars' vicious attitude toward the Christians, living or dead. Often the Fossores, in order to secure the remains of a Christian martyr, found themselves obliged to risk their own life, by sneaking into a Roman "dead-house" where, following the Christians' torture and execution, their corpses were left to decay. . . . If the Fossores were discovered, Roman law imposed the penalty of death upon them.[2]

The Fossores were the forerunners of today's funeral directors. In Christian tradition, the church was responsible for the care of the dead, at least after the construction of church buildings began. The Gospels report the experience of the women followers going to the tomb to complete the anointing of Jesus's body (they had been forced to stop because of the approach of Sabbath).

Centuries later, family or friends "laid out" the corpse (often in the residence) and, at least unofficially, certified the individual was dead. In Tudor and Stuart England, "poor women were often employed to sit by someone dying, to watch by the corpse [while family members got some sleep], and to clean it and prepare it for burial." Often, neighbor women and female servants were recruited to clean the corpse. In some cases, midwives "as adept at laying out as lying in" took on this responsibility.[3] Thomas Lynch comments:

This was a dour and awful choice, moving the dead from place to place. And like most chores, it was left to the women to do. Later, it was discovered to be a high honor—to *bear the pall* as a liturgical role required a special place in the procession, special conduct, and often a really special outfit. When hauling the dead hither and yon became less a chore and more an honor, men took it over with enthusiasm. [4]

In the 1880s individuals began to use caskets for burials, so building caskets became a sideline for many furniture makers. Over time, as the American economy grew, individuals wanted nicer caskets, so casket manufacturing developed in urban areas.

The individual who "undertook" to make the arrangements for the family became the undertaker. The Civil War made embalming more common (in order to ship soldiers' bodies home). At that point emerged the mortician, who embalmed the body.

As a result of the urban expansion, homes and apartments were smaller. So the mortician began offering space for the visitation and the funeral in a parlor (often one room in his house). Soon the funeral home became a fixture in the community. Over time, fewer and fewer visitations and funerals were held in the primary residence.

Given the number of details to be managed, the mortician or undertaker became the funeral director of today.

Q116 Are there many women funeral directors?

Women have long been involved in funeral service; admittedly, many were the wives, daughters, or daughters-in-law of funeral home owners. Currently, more than half of the students enrolled in mortuary education programs are female.[1]

I believe a female funeral director enhances a funeral service. Kathy Ordiway, a funeral director, explains the role of women in the profession:

> Some families are more comfortable expressing their feelings to a female. Especially in deaths of children. A lot of people see the males as the "business persons" and females as the "listening persons." At times men feel it's okay to cry with a woman but feel they need to be strong in front of the male staff.[2]

Q117 How much training does it take to be a
       funeral director?
Training varies according to state requirements. Four states
require that a licensed funeral director be a college graduate;
most states require some level of college. All licensed funeral
directors and embalmers are required to pass an examination. In
some states a funeral director must also be licensed as an
embalmer. The National Funeral Directors Association and
other mortuary groups provide extensive continuing education
programs as well.

Q118 Isn't the funeral industry a big rip-off?
       Don't funeral directors take advantage of
       your vulnerability at the time of death?
Certainly, Jessica Mitford's book, *The American Way of Death,* pro-
motes such a perception. Unfortunately, she and other critics have
used a broad brush to indict an entire profession for the ethical
lapses and choices of a few. Name a profession that does not have
"bad apples" or some practitioners who are not committed to
maintaining the highest standards of service and professionalism.
    The idea of a funeral service as a rip-off is ridiculous. With
2.3 million human beings dying in America each year, families
need trained, caring professionals to bury their dead with dignity. I did not say "dispose" of the dead. (There are "efficient"
alternatives being offered, some of which, believe me, you do not
want to encounter.) Moreover, a do-it-yourself burial movement is evolving in some areas of the country. Some argue that
if we can have midwives in the birthing process, why not "thana-
tological midwives" in the burying process.
    Admittedly, a traditional funeral is a major expenditure
especially when unplanned. Yet consider what is spent on wed-
dings in this country—especially in light of a one in two failure
rate. The Conde Nast Bridal Infobank, a research service, says
the average wedding in the United States costs $22,000.[1] No one

complains (well, maybe the father of the bride) about what is spent. Yet, funerals, which cost significantly less than the average wedding, are sources of agitation by activists. Some wail about all that money going "into a hole in the ground"!

If you think it's a rip-off, you've never met my friends who are funeral directors. You've never waited on dinner with them because they are attending the needs of other families. You have never seen them yawn at breakfast because they have been up half the night making a body look acceptable to the family (when some would have just said, "Close the casket").

Funeral professionals work hard to "be there" for families and friends. They deserve to make a good living. For many directors, funeral service is a ministry and many of their acts of charity go unnoticed and underappreciated.

Yes, it is possible to spend a lot of money for a casket that is going into a grave—not just any "hole in the ground." But then walk through the funeral home parking lot and check out the vehicles of families. Yes, someone who drives up in an Explorer or Navigator or does three weeks at their condo in Hawaii may spend a lot for a funeral. Yes, some families do spend more than they have to spend or should spend. But they also do that for birthdays, graduations, and anniversaries.

Few individuals really want to go out "cheap." Doug Manning's father often grumbled, "Just put me in a pine box and throw me in some ditch," a sentiment which Doug concludes "all men seem to feel the need" to say. Finally, Doug challenged his father's thinking. "I told him the funeral was my gift to him and, if he did not mind, I would decide what kind of gift I would give him."[2]

Q119 What about directors who offer discount funeral services?

As funeral costs have increased—and public concern about the costs has spiraled—discounters have found a niche in a consumer society that says, "if you paid full price, you paid too much." The discount mentality has affected almost every component of our economy. The average funeral cost for an adult in 2002 was $6,876, not counting cemetery expenses and incidentals.[1] Obviously, there are lots of funerals (by the time all expenses are calculated) that exceed that.

There are individuals who want a bargain and shop around for the best deal. Some individuals have challenged or dysfunctional relationships, or even nonexistent emotional relationships, with the deceased. So their focus may be entirely on the bottom line: "What is it going to cost?"

There are also the "vigilante consumers." They want "speed, convenience, choice, value, and to be appreciated" and are often impatient, according to consumer specialist Patricia Fripp.[2]

Some families struggle with the costs. Historically, funeral homes generally carried their own financial paper so that a person would make a down payment and gradually pay off the note. Now, few funeral homes operate on other than a payment-at-time-of-services. Which of your credit cards would you use if you had to pay for even an average-costing funeral? Given the debt of many individuals and families, economies can be realized. For example, do you need to ride to the cemetery in a limousine? Could the pallbearers drive themselves? How long an obituary (in cities where newspapers charge for obituaries) is needed? Would a "cyber" obituary on the Internet be a wiser investment? How many nights of visitation should you have? Funeral discounters fulfill an important service in today's economy, especially with families who have limited financial resources.

Q120 My parents have a preneed arrangement for their funerals and burials. It is wise to pay for the funeral ahead of time?

Some individuals are planners. They plan ahead for all of life's eventualities. Some are "controllers" even from the grave. Many individuals believe by preplanning and prepaying they are saving their family the headaches of making decisions after their death.

Preplanning says, "This is what I want." Many families are overwhelmed in making arrangements because they "never talked about it" with their loved ones. They plan rituals and memorialization although without knowing specific wishes. That can distract them from their grief work because they keep reassessing decisions, "Did I do the right thing?"

I would suggest leaving a few details unplanned. This gives family members a vehicle for jump-starting discussions (although it does leave the family open to differences and disputes).

Even if a funeral is preplanned, these days, given the family realities, some family member may wish to set aside a stated decision of the deceased. That challenge can create issues for other family members who insist, "But that is what she/he wanted."

If you do wish to preplan and/or prepay, like any contract you sign, read the fine print. Ask questions. Given the mobility of Americans, be cautious about boundary restrictions in preneed contracts. For example, suppose as a retiree, you die in Florida and have a preneed policy with a Florida mortuary. Your family decides on a funeral and burial back home in Maine. Will that preneed policy transfer? Suppose you bought a casket and later decide you want to be cremated and scattered? Is all of your money refundable?

Remember also that prepaid plans will not necessarily cover all the costs. Christine Dugas points out the price of floral arrangements or newspaper obituaries may have increased over time, so your contract actually buys less. If you decide to "lock in" a price, also make certain that 100 percent of the funds are held in trust by a bank that is FDIC insured.

Dugas suggests, "Many funeral planners suggest writing your preferences, setting aside funds to pay for the funeral in a particular bank account, and notifying the executor of your estate."[1]

Keep the contract with your will, but also keep a copy assessable to your executor. Make certain that your next-of-kin know where key documents are located. Go over the document(s) with your family members, or a designated family member, so that there is clarity "when the time comes."

Unfortunately, there are people who plan every single detail of their own funeral. They might be called "postmortem control freaks."

I deal with family members who have not spoken in years because of something that happened in planning or carrying out the funeral arrangements. In some families, the adage about cooking comes to mind: too many cooks spoil the ritual.

Q121 How can I know that my wishes for rituals will be carried out?

Put your desires in writing. Let your family and friends know your wishes. Ask for verbal assurances that they will follow your wishes. Some individuals teasingly threaten: "I will come back and haunt you if you do not do what I want." Be cautious in the selection of your executor. One individual wrote Ann Landers: "Please tell your readers NEVER to trust someone else to carry out their wishes without specifying those wishes in black and white."[1] That's good advice.

18. Questions about Cremation

> "One of the more perplexing problems funeral homes
> encounter is what to do with unclaimed cremains."
> —*T. Scott Gilligan*[1]

> "The bishops [of the Catholic Church] say the cremated
> remains of a body should be treated with the same respect
> given to the corporeal remains of a human being.
> This includes the matter in which they are carried,
> the care and attention to the appropriate placement
> and transport and final disposition."
> —*James P. Moroney*[2]

Q122 A friend insists that cremation is pagan. Is it permissible for Christians to be cremated?

Cremation is a growing choice for many Christians. In 2001, cremation was used in 27.78 percent of all deaths.[1] In several Western states, cremation is chosen by the majority—as it is in many urban areas and areas with high concentrations of retirees.

Some individuals have strong feelings against cremation; some have religious objections. However, there is nothing in the New Testament that explicitly says cremation is wrong, although how individuals "interpret" a particular scripture might support their opinion. Cremation should not be seen as a pagan tradition any more than embalming is; after all, the Egyptians mastered the embalming process several millennia ago.

In time, all bodies will decompose, some faster than others. Cremation is a controlled, accelerated decomposition.

Q123 What should I do with the ashes?

First, human remains are not "ashes." Ashes are what you have in your fireplace or grill after a fire. Human remains are *cremated remains*. Admittedly, that phrase may be difficult to say the first couple of times, but it is a way of respecting the dead.

Second, the cremated remains should be treated with the same respect that you would show a corpse. In fact, the Roman Catholic Church requires that the cremated remains be committed to the soil or to the water. They should not be placed, or left, in a bedroom closet or in the trunk of a car.

Third, the decision regarding what to do with the cremated remains should be planned as you would plan for a burial. Cremation offers a potential for denial and postponement. Many grievers do not immediately pick up their loved ones' cremated remains. Other mourners delay scattering or committing the cremated remains because that will "finalize" their loss.

Q124 Is it wrong to scatter?

It is not so much a matter of being "wrong" but well advised. Certainly, some individuals wish to be "scattered" in a place that had significant meaning to them; a few wish to be scattered in multiple places. Hopefully, they have communicated those wishes clearly to survivors.

Who can forget the pictures of the Kennedy and Bissette families aboard the USS *Briscoe*, on July 22, 1999? They scattered their loved ones' cremated remains near the spot where John F. Kennedy Jr.'s plane crashed into the Atlantic. Such pictures influence trends.

Technically, you need permission to scatter cremated remains on the property of another person or on federal or state property. In practice, many use the adage, "It is easier to ask for forgiveness than for permission."

As more people choose cremation as an alternative to traditional burial, the disposal of the remains is getting more attention. *The New York Times* recently reported that residents of Venice on the Bay in Pasadena, Maryland, were taking a stand against outsiders sprinkling cremated human remains on their small local beach where people would wade and swim.[1]

Grievers should ponder: "How can we fulfill this responsibility with dignity?" It should not be a "Well, that's done" task. Some want a clergy person involved; some families or friends decide to do a brief ritual or service themselves.

If scattering is chosen, I recommend not to scatter all the cremated remains; bury some. Why? Future generations need a place to come on special days. The "she's out here somewhere" is too vague for some family members and friends.

Q125 How long should cremated remains be kept?

Herein lies the problem, as Detective Lt. Columbo would say. Some individuals delay disposition of the cremated remains as a way of avoiding the finality of the death. Some individuals will never get around to it. Later, their own executors have been surprised to find a box and ask, "What's this?"

There are no time restrictions on keeping cremated remains. Yet you will want to make plans for how you wish to honor your loved one in the same way that you would have planned for a burial.

Illnesses and other conflicts may prevent some extended family members from attending a funeral right away. Travel expenses may prohibit others from going. While the airlines offer "bereavement fares" for those needing to travel quickly to funerals, these fares are based on the top-of-the-line prices. Cremation allows families to plan a ceremony to bury or scatter the cremated remains months out, perhaps around a family occasion or reunion. This way, air travel can be purchased at cheaper prices, and families can budget for the expense.

Cremation offers extended families the opportunity to gather several months after the death.

It is important to talk the possibilities over with family members rather than making a unilateral decision. Balance their opinions with the wishes or the presumed wishes of the deceased.

Q126 Doesn't cremation save the land for the living?

"Saving the land for the living" has been a slogan bantered around as a motivation for cremation. Yet cemeteries are not "land for the dead" but sacred spaces for memorialization. No one seems to complain about devoting land to building another golf course or strip mall in the suburbs.

Certainly cremation is very efficient in the use of land, given the number of cremated remains that can be committed in the same space as a traditional burial plot. Cremation does help facilitate burial in some national cemeteries that no longer accept casketed remains because of a shortage of space.

Q127 Isn't cremation just a way to save money?

Unfortunately, for some decision makers it all comes down to the bottom line, especially when there was a strained or dysfunctional relationship with the deceased. Cremation is less expensive, but it is not necessarily inexpensive. According to the 1999 Wirthlin Report, 24 percent of respondents reported cost to be the major factor in the decision for cremation; 17 percent said they made the decision because cremation uses less land, and 13 percent said cremation was less emotional and more convenient.[1]

Q128 How do I explain cremation to young children?

As cremation becomes more common, particularly in areas where it has been less acceptable, many children will have questions. Alan Wolfelt, Director of the Center for Grief and Loss Transition, offers three pieces of advice:

- ↝ Follow the child's lead. The child will teach you what he/she is curious about.
- ↝ Give only as much information as the child wants to know.
- ↝ Give children honest answers in words they understand.

In reality, many adults have the same questions about the cremation process but never ask. Many adults are at a loss, or are uncomfortable, receiving questions on cremation from children. Here's some information Wolfelt calls "child-friendly:"

- ↝ There is no smell or smoke when a body is cremated. The heat burns away all the parts of the body except some pieces of bone.
- ↝ After cremation, what is left of the body looks like the small rocks at the bottom of a fish bowl; it is white because it is bone.

- When a body is buried in the ground, it breaks down over months and years until just a skeleton is left. Cremation makes that happen much, much faster.
- Cremation has been used for thousands of years.
- Cremation does not hurt. The person is dead, which means the body does not work any more. Its heart does not beat, its brain has stopped working, it does not breathe, and it does not feel anything any more.[1]

Children may ask questions in waves. Your answer to an initial question may be satisfactory. The child may have another question in days, weeks, or months. The important thing is maintaining a relationship so that a child can bring questions to you.

19. Questions about Memorialization

> "We need our witnesses and archivists to say we lived,
> we died, we made this difference."
> —*Thomas Lynch*[1]

Q129 My sister goes to my brother-in-law's grave several times a week even though he has been dead for nine months. What is her problem?

Many professionals and grievers would not consider visiting the grave often a problem. Living at the grave might be, but not visiting. Visiting the grave is a way to practice remembering.

For some, it takes a long time of interacting with a grave to come to the full realization that a loved one is dead. Admittedly, some individuals never go. As one woman snapped in my grief group, "He's *not* there! Why would I go to the grave?" Over the years, I have learned that grievers have different feelings; some would agree with this sentiment, others would not, and many are too early in grief to have made up their mind.

For a brief period in college, I lived in a cemetery. I got to know some of the regulars: the husband who came every Tuesday afternoon, the wives and mothers who came in the mornings, those who came on Sundays like clockwork. George Burns went to Gracie's grave every week, and no one said he had "a problem." Burns explained that it was a place where he could tell her things.

Sometimes individuals go to cemeteries because the key individuals in their lives—even in their families—are not listening to their expressions of grief. Or they are not listening to the ends of their sentences. They have already moved on and want the chief mourner to move on, too. One woman told me that going to the cemetery was "just a good place to get things off my chest."

In the days before cemeteries offered perpetual care (the permanent caring for the grave and surrounding cemetery grounds), families or friends "tended" the grave. Actually, that gave them a reason—or an acceptable explanation—to go to the grave. These days, the level of perpetual care can vary; some individuals take clippers or cleaning products when they go to the cemetery

Many find cemeteries safe places to cry. No one thrusts a tissue or handkerchief at them.

to tidy up the grave. Memorial Day was originally called Decoration Day. Mourners "decorated" the graves with flowers. The day also facilitated the spring cleaning of graveyards.

Remember, for centuries, graveyards surrounded churches. In some settings, individuals were buried inside the church (in the floors or walls). Now, through cremation and columbariums, that practice is being restored.

Some grievers do go to the grave or burial site a lot. For a while, Jackie Kennedy visited the president's grave at Arlington

National Cemetery three times a day. If you have a "problem" with someone's need to visit a grave, keep it to yourself. Your concern will sound like criticism. The last thing she needs at the moment is criticism.

Q130 My mother's second husband has not gotten around to buying a grave marker for her. Should I take care of this?

Some cemeteries, to get around this issue, offer temporary markers until a permanent marker can be chosen and installed. Many grievers find the temporary sign troubling or a "burr in the saddle."

Your mother's husband could be facing some financial difficulties he does not want to admit. The "right" marker can be a significant expenditure on top of what has already been spent. Or he may be stalling in handling this detail as a way of avoiding the striking finality of a marker. When my father was interred, my mother had her name ("Mary C. Smith, 1916–___") carved in the mausoleum marble as well. I lost track of how many times I saw that. But it was unsettling the first time I saw "Mary C. Smith, 1916–*1999*." For some the marker is a significant encounter with finality.

Think out your concerns about the lack of a monument. Talk to your siblings. Then speak to your mother's husband. You might offer, "We would like to contribute to this gift of memory for our mother."

When you plan the marker, consider engraving the exact dates of her birth and death rather than just the years. The avoidance of specifics has been another way to delimit the reality of death. Your loved one had a birthday *and* your loved one had a death date. Honor both.

Q131 As a widow, I married a widower whose
       children have been tolerant but not overly
       accepting of me. Since my children are by
       my first husband, I would like to be buried
       next to him. How do I tell this to my current
       husband, who keeps saying we need to buy
       cemetery plots?

I commend your husband for talking about this important
detail. You could continue to stall this conversation and hope
you outlive him; thus he will never know. Or you could go ahead
and buy the plots but not buy a common marker. You could
offer a delay tactic, "One thing at a time." It is not like the "other"
grave will go wanting. Some families need a space for a child or
grandchild (regardless of the age). But again, you are risking that
your current husband will die first.

   The difficult choice would be to talk it out, though your
husband may already sense your wishes in your reluctance to
attend to this important decision. Visiting cemeteries can be a
way of informally talking aloud about our wishes.

   This problem is not new. One time when visiting my pater-
nal great-grandfather's grave, I noticed he had been married
three times (which I did not know before). I looked at the markers to the right and left. I commented to my mother, who was
with me, "It says he was married three times." My mother nod-
ded. "Well, here is wife number one, and there is wife number
two. Where is wife number three?"

   My mother looked around a moment. "Well, she is here
somewhere. I remember her funeral. I bet she is buried with her
first husband." And she was.

Q132 My seventeen-year-old daughter died days after her high school graduation. I still keep up her pictures because they comfort me. Whenever my mother-in-law visits she throws a fit saying the pictures depress her. Should I put away the pictures when she comes to visit?

When I visit a home, I notice where and how family pictures are displayed. Pictures are a wonderful way to express our lives and loves. Pictures of loved ones who have died also help us keep our grief.

Nothing bothers me more than those who want to purge a residence of the pictures of the deceased.

I believe in displaying these pictures. My mother kept a picture of my father on the dresser in the bedroom. Whenever something bothered her, or she wondered what to do, she went and "talked" to the picture. It worked for her.

One Sunday morning I was flipping through religious TV-land and heard a televangelist snarl, "Get those pictures off the wall! We don't worship the dead! We serve a living God." I resisted the immediate temptation to dial the 800 number in the lower screen by reminding myself, "He has never lost anyone." But I was troubled that some of his "followers" may have taken down pictures.

A photograph—which is really just a piece of paper—does not have the power to make anyone depressed. Losing a granddaughter does. Trying to limit the impact of that loss does. This is a case when *su casa* is not your mother-in-law's *casa*. Keep the pictures out and up (and keep some on lower levels so that children can easily see them).

Q133 After my fifteen-year-old grandson died in a tragic boating accident, my daughter-in-law "embalmed" his bedroom. Everything is just like he left it—nothing has been touched in four years. It's morbid. Should I confront her or hope she will grow out of this?

I am more concerned about those who "sweep and cleanse" the bedroom immediately than those who wait to deal with the effects. The death of a child, particularly an "almost-raised" child, is one of life's harshest realities for a parent. Some parents are enraged that the world goes on, particularly for their child's siblings and friends. Parents may feel powerless over the death, but the child's bedroom is something they do have power over. In a society that does not want them to cling to their grief, they tend this space privately.

Mary Todd Lincoln never went into the bedroom in the White House where her son Willie died in 1863 or to the Green Room where he was laid out. President Abraham Lincoln, on the other hand, often went to that room to sit and reflect on the loss. Admittedly, many times in the early months, it offered him a safe place to weep out of sight of his aides.[1]

In cases such as yours, I would urge close friends and family members to offer to help with the effects. In many cases, grieving parents claim they want to do it alone or on their own time. You can say, "Whenever you want some help, just call me."

For some family members, seeing the deceased's "stuff" stuffed into black plastic bags and dumped in the garbage, is troubling. When parents are ready, some prefer to box and store the personal items. Others allow friends of their son or daughter to select items. Many parents have found it helpful to have someone there to listen to the stories that particular objects launch.

Give your daughter-in-law some more time. It could be she has a horrendous fear that this son is going to be forgotten in a "move-on-and-get-over-it" world. These objects and this space give her permission to remember.

20. Questions about Wills and Estates

"Nearly 60 percent of adult Americans do not have wills. . . .
If you die intestate, or without a will, what happens
to your estate—and in some cases, the well-being of your
survivors—may be decided by strangers in state courts."
—*Susan Stellin*[1]

"Big memories can reside in the wooden chocolate-pudding
spoon, and value is in the sentimental eye of the beholder."
—*Joyce Madelon Winslow*[2]

"For the most part the American legal system—
with its annoying penchant for impenetrable language
spewed out of computer programs with seemingly
inexhaustible supplies of murky phrases—has taken most
of the fun out of wills. What we get now are wills like mine,
with subsections galore but no spark of life."
—*Bill Tammeus*[3]

Q134 Why do I need a will?

In 2000, Americans inherited close to $150 billion, according to the Boston College Social Welfare Research Institute. Moreover, during the next fifty years, an estimated $30 trillion is projected to pass from one generation to the next in the United States.[1]

Every adult needs a will. Jane Bryant Quinn, a respected financial adviser, explains that three "immutable facts" support having a will: "You own stuff. You will die. Someone will get that stuff."[2] Great truth is found in the saying, "Where there's a will, there's a way." Where there is *not* a will, there can be chaos.

Families promise a lot of things to dying individuals; however, the will is a way to enforce your wishes. For example, even if everyone knew you wished to be cremated, one family member may protest, even block, that wish, and other family members, "to make peace," may go along with it. "Only with a will," says estate planner Andy Morrison, "can you control exactly who will get what, when, and how."[3]

> A will is a way to make certain, or reasonably certain, your wishes for disposing of what you own and what you value will be honored.

Gays, lesbians, and unmarried heterosexuals in long-term relationships especially need wills to protect their intentions. Since such relationships are legally sanctioned only in certain states, the right to dispose of an estate falls to blood relatives, who may or may not honor a deceased's wishes if there has not been legal preparation. Some partners have found themselves evicted from their own residences by the family.

Some of the most devastated widows I have worked with are those whose husbands died intestate (without a valid will). Incredible numbers of individuals die with outdated wills that no longer represent their intentions or the best interests of all their survivors. Some people divorce and remarry without altering their wills, then when they die, the existing will distributes the assets to an ex-spouse! That alone should be reason for every divorced person to review wills. And remember, you may be worth more dead than alive if you die in an "at fault" loss like a plane crash or a tragedy like the World Trade Center disaster.

Wills are something a lot of individuals intend "to get around to." Unfortunately, some individuals run out of time and those they love inherit the consequences. Without a will, the legal expenses can eat into the corpus of an estate and greatly complicate the grief of your survivors. In some cases, a second family (or third) can be left destitute by an inadequate will.

Do yourself, your family, your friends, your charities, and your executor a big favor: Have a will and make sure your executor knows where the document is located. Periodically review the will to make certain it reflects your wishes. If you fail to write a will, the state will, in essence, write one for you—and your survivors may not care for it!

Q135 My siblings have not spoken since the will was read. This estrangement would have broken my parents' hearts. How can I bring about reconciliation?

You never know what kind of family you are in until you divide an estate. Some who protest, "Oh, my family would *never* argue over stuff," may be in for one big surprise. I caution individuals, "Don't be so sure about that." One family argued over a treasured heirloom quilt. They ended up cutting the quilt in quarters so each sister would have a part of the quilt.

For some, the contents of the will can be a surprise or an ambush. Suppose family members and charities had been led to believe than an estate would be divided three ways. What was implied was "three *equally* divided ways." But does the will state that?

You may need to convene a "conference of the family" to discuss the consequences of the will: financial and social. You may need the tenacity and diplomacy of Colin Powell to soothe feelings and expectations. In some cases, an unequal distribution affects future generations as much as current generations.

An old expression says, "Possession is nine-tenths of the law." Some items "disappear" in families following a death, even though "it was here when mother died." Sadly, sometimes old family issues get rebooted in the settlement of an estate.

Q136 I always thought that all my mother's possessions were to be divided equally. When the will was probated, my sister got two-thirds. My husband says, "Forget about it." What should I do about my sister's greediness?

Sometimes, family members are at a loss to understand the reasoning a parent used in constructing provisions of a will. You call it "greediness," but are you certain your sister's fingerprints are on your mother's will? Maybe your mother had a reason for that stipulation of distribution.

It's easy to say, "It's just money," or "It's just stuff." But it doesn't take a boulder in the shoe to make us uncomfortable. Many individuals have followed the advice of your husband.

You will have to decide if you can live with your sister's largess. She may be as surprised by the terms of the will as you; she may be as in the dark to a why as you.

Q137 My children will fight over the money and antiques. Who should I choose to be my executor?

Choosing an executor is one of the most important decisions you will make. Under legal supervision of a probate court, executors gather your assets; pay debts, taxes, funeral, and cemetery expenses; and deal with the distribution of your possessions according to the directions of *your* will. Handing the details of even a moderate estate can be a Herculean task.

While it is common practice to select a family member, an individual may be wise to rethink that choice depending on their family circumstances. Greg Owens, a financial planner and accountant who has worked with many families, writes, "Do not pass up a nonfamily executor simply because there is a fee involved. Often the conflict of interest or the contests that result by naming a family member can be far more costly to the estate than the fees charged by an outsider."[1]

Consider a corporate executive, a bank or trust company, or a professional accountant or lawyer or investment advisor. Explain to your children why you selected an outsider. Some may silently rejoice at that decision.

21. Questions about Support

"In the past few years since Frank's death I have
become part of a secret society, a club of widows
and widowers who feel safe to share their stories of loss
and mourning and grief and their special secrets.
Sometimes that club includes parents who have lost
a child, a son grieving for his father, a gay man coping
with the death of a twenty-five-year partner.
I have heard many secrets from those facing
the loss of a loved one. Repeatedly, people will preface
their secrets with, 'I know this will sound weird . . .'"
—*Barbara K. Roberts*[1]

"Why would you want to hear other people's stories?
So I can have permission to tell my own."
—*Susan Ford Wiltshire*[2]

Q138 What about friends who made promises at the visitation, "Just let me know if there is any way I can help"? No one seems available to help me. Why do I have to ask for help?

Ever heard the cliché, "People mean well?" Sometimes the offers of support were just clichés mumbled because the speaker did not know what else to say. One widow complained, "No one ever says 'no' outrightly. They just never seem very enthusiastic about helping." Eventually some grievers tire of asking for help. Significant changes in levels of support have led Robert Neimeyer to conclude that survivors "construct and reconstruct their identities as survivors *in negotiation* with *others.*" (author's emphasis)[1] Grievers have to ask and to re-ask.

The psalmist lamented on the reality, "Do not be far from me, for trouble is near and there is no one to help" (Psalm 22:11). Many who promised support have some hint of an expectation for how long your grief should last. If you do not grieve on their timetable, they are less likely to be supportive.

One elderly widow told me, "It's at times like this that you learn who your real friends are."

Q139 Friends were so good about offering help in the first weeks after my husband died. Now some friends treat me as if I have the plague. How do I convince them that I am not after their husbands?

Compassion is not a long suit for lots of individuals—particularly those who have never experienced grief firsthand. Some are good for transitional or initial compassionate care. Subconsciously, they do not want to "reward" individuals who do not follow their expectations for grief recovery.

Barbara Bartocci says, "Try and forgive those who drop away. Realize that it's not you they're rejecting, but your circumstances."[1] While I agree with Bartocci, it is easier to convince your head of that reality than your heart. Through the experience of grief you will have three surprises: those friends who will distance themselves, those who offer unexpectedly gracious care, and those who will become your new friends.

Q140 My adult children want me to sell my home and move into a condo. I am not ready to do that. What should I tell them?

This is a common tension between adult children and a grieving mother or father. Some children assume you will be overwhelmed by the memories in this home, or by the maintenance or security. Most grievers, however, find a home to be a safe place initially to grieve. Many find the memories of space and place comforting. In time, you may want to downsize, so that you will have less to clean or take care of (or insure or heat or cool).

Give major decisions time.

Consider what your children have to say but make decisions based on your own wisdom. The conventional advice that has been appreciated by legions of grievers has been: Make no major decisions in the first year. Too many widows and widowers have been talked into housing decisions—and other decisions—they later come to regret.

22. Questions about Responsibility for Griever Care

> "Be as gentle with yourself as you are with your loved one."
> —*Barbara Bartocci*[1]

Q141 Since my father-in-law died, my mother-in-law has become helpless. She cannot make the simplest decision without calling—at all hours of the day and night—to ask my husband's advice. What can I do?

After a death, some grievers are in grief-shock, not unlike the traumatic-shock soldiers experience in wartime. In families where traditional male/female roles and responsibilities are absolute, many widows are apprehensive about facing demands their husbands handled, such as balancing a checkbook or changing the filters in a furnace or getting an oil change for the car. (Yet other widows have been empowered by the new sense of freedom.)

Some of your mother-in-law's requests may be disguising a request for attention. Under the guise of getting advice, she gets a moment of her son's time. She may be hesitant to call and say,

"I'm lonely," or "I'm missing your father." Some projects she could perhaps do alone give her a chance to create "project intimacy" with family members. While the work goes on, a story gets told, a memory gets nurtured. She may say things like "Remember how your dad hated raking leaves?" or "Do you remember the time the bottom of the bag broke and leaves blew everywhere?" Or conversation may flow in the moments after a chore, when she says, "Let me fix you something to eat."

Sometimes primary requests for help are masking secondary requests or concerns. Your mother-in-law may be bugging her son to repair an exterior light, yet underlying this request, she is really feeling unsafe being alone in her home. She may be asking for help with her bank papers, but really she is worried about her financial situation.

Family dynamics become tightened and stressed when an in-law considers the requests for assistance excessive. You did not say if your husband is an only child, or if he is the child who lives closest to the mother, or if he is the child who can "manage" mom. Sometimes, a son or daughter has to say "no." Sometimes, assistance initially seen as transitional becomes a permanent expectation.

You may consider locating a retired person who is available to help your mother-in-law on a per hour basis. Paying someone else to do "handy work" may prove to be a good investment.

Q142 Because I am not married, some of my siblings expect me to take care of my widowed mother. They hint that she should come and live with me or that I should move back home. I have a life and a career. I am willing to do my fair share, but how do I say no to their expectations?

Many unmarried adults can identify with this issue. In some families, this is almost an ingrained expectation that can be expressed in the phrase, "since you do not have a family of your own." Yet not all adults can share space with a parent, particularly on the parent's turf. And as life-expectancy rates soar, the issues of how to care for aging parents will only become more complex.

Tight job markets also complicate the scenario. Some adult children have to travel, or be open to traveling, in their jobs. Given downsizing and the realities of the economy, some family members are forced to relocate to keep jobs. As a single adult, you have to think of your economic future and job security too.

Fortunate are those in "We're in this thing together" type families.

Consider holding a family discussion on this issue. Sometimes it's helpful to limit participation to siblings and/or the surviving parent. It may be difficult to have a full, candid discussion of the issues or the anticipated issues. Remember, you do not need to defend yourself, but you may need to educate your family about your life. Have the conversation before an emergency develops. Stand your ground.

I have seen individuals who have given up their lives and their careers to shoulder a family's responsibility for an aged parent. I have met some embittered, angry single adults. Whatever you do, you need time for you.

23. Questions about Grief in the Workplace

"Hidden grief costs U.S. companies
more than $75 billion annually."
—*Grief Recovery Institute*[1]

"His boss acted differently around him now, and so did his
coworkers. They trod gently outside his office and would
stop a few feet from his desk, as if, should they be too
relaxed in his presence, what had happened to him would
happen to them—as if having a dead child were
contagious. No one knew how he did what he did,
while simultaneously they wanted him to shut
all signs of his grief away."
—*Alice Sebold*[2]

"Because so many people spend so much time at their
workplace and develop strong relationships with fellow
workers, the workplace is a vital place for recovery."
—*Johnette Hartnett*[3]

Q143 How long before a grieving individual should go back to work?

Some individuals want to go back to work immediately. They see work as a refuge or distraction from the grief. Russell Friedman, co-director of the Grief Recovery Institute, recommends ten days. "When your heart is broken, your head doesn't work right."[1]

It comes, then, as no surprise that a significant percentage of workplace accidents, according to Jeff Zaslow, are grief related, due to an inability to focus. Don Lee, who went back to work two days after his daughter's funeral (she had been struck by a drunk driver and had been on life support for fifty-four days), explains, "I put in my full eight-hour day, but for six months, I didn't do more than four hours of work each day."[2]

In some cases, the question of "how long" is answered by an employer's bereavement leave. Ninety-two percent of employers provide paid bereavement leave—usually four days or less.

The real issue is what circumstances are allowed by bereavement policies. Some policies cover only the immediate next of kin: father, mother, spouse, child. Other policies add siblings. Many companies do not cover the new definitions of family: stepfamily members. For example, given the age of parents, your mother may have had three husbands. You may consider her current husband to be "Dad" or a stepparent. So, what happens when he dies?

Bereavement policies often do not take geographic mobility into consideration. An employee may receive three days or five days of leave, but it takes a day to fly or drive there and another to get back. In essence, the employee spends bereavement leave just getting to and from the funeral.

Some grievers, unfortunately, feel pressure to return to work prematurely due to financial concerns. They need money to handle the out-of-pocket expenses of attending the funeral (airfares, motel, car rental, meals), or there may be an expectation to contribute to funeral expenses.

Other grievers may have to return to work immediately because of instability in the workplace: "My job is on the line." Layoffs or downsizing may be imminent at their company, and time away may be seen as weakness.

Ironically, some companies have cut bereavement leave as a way of controlling costs. Legally the bereavement leave may be there but a good "team" player will not take all of it.

Finally, a critical factor is the type of work you do. Many individuals travel extensively in their jobs; upon returning to work, they may be hundreds (or thousands) of miles from their homes. In the evenings, they are not physically with family members in their grief. A hotel room with room service and cable in a strange city is not conducive to grief, nor is the bar in the lobby or down the street.

Talk over the decision with your immediate supervisor and human resources. Remember, some may say, "Take all the time you need," but not mean it.

Q144 My coworkers are afraid to say anything to me. Some want to know why I am still grieving since my mother had been ill for so long. What do I do with my grief in the workplace?

When Jesus said, "Blessed are those who mourn, for they will be comforted" (Matthew 5:4), he did not add, *"in the workplace."* Few business environments are griever-friendly; most are unsafe places for individuals committed to doing thorough grief work.

Your colleagues, who sent the nice floral piece and signed the beautiful sympathy card, may not know what to say when you come back to work. Some may avoid you or keep interaction "strictly business." However, you may be pleasantly surprised by a colleague, one you may not even know, who drops by, sends a note or an e-mail, and says, "I am thinking about you. If you ever need someone to talk to, let me know."

Sooner or later someone else will be the "new griever on the block." Lobbying for compassion may not benefit you, but it may benefit the next griever in your workplace.

Q145 My supervisor insists my work performance has suffered since my husband's illness and death. How can I convince my supervisor that I have a right to "still" be grieving?

I am teaching a university course, "Grief in the Workplace," that hopefully will prepare future managers to be more compassionate. But individuals can earn a prestigious MBA and still be ignorant about bereavement until it happens to them. The reality is "if you haven't been there, you don't understand." Johnette Harnett in her book, *Grief in the Workplace: 40 Hours Plus Overtime* warns, "Remember your boss probably knows less about suicide and grief than you do."[1]

Check out your company's Employee Assistance Program, if one is available. They might provide some resources or a counselor. You might find it wise to ask for a temporary reassignment.

In some cases, the supervisor's or colleague's job might be on the line, so she is just passing along the stress. I wish we had little yellow signs "Griever Zone" that we could post on workstations or offices. You might want to ask the person: Who have you lost? (How you ask the question might influence the answer.) In reality, your supervisor or colleague may have had a significant loss and has, up to this point, kept an "out of sight, out of mind" stance. Your grief is rebooting her grief or anticipated grief.

Your grief could be a learning experience for others.

Again, Harnett points out, "Unless an employee works in

total isolation, his grief will have some affect on his fellow employees."[2] Yes, death can make shambles of work performance. I think that is good. What should trouble us is "business as usual" following a death.

Q146 As a parent who must travel for business, how do I cope with the threat of a terrorist attack?

You may want to evaluate the "must" in your question. You may want to cutback. The events of September 11, 2001, have caused many individuals and their employers to reevaluate the need for travel and procedures for safe travel.

Family or friends should know your itinerary while traveling or going "on the road." (This is important in any case. Without leaving word with loved ones, incredible efforts are sometimes needed to track down business travelers or vacationers or retirees to receive news of a death of a family member or friend.) How are you traveling—plane, car, bus, train? When are you going? When are coming back? Where are you staying? What are your phone numbers?

Cell phones have been an incredible enhancement to notification and reassurance. Families and friends should also set up alternative notification methods. "If something happens, each of us will call 'X,'" says Susan in Milwaukee.

Make certain your family and your executor know where important documents are located: insurance policies, deeds, will, living will, medical power of attorney in health care matters, tax records, birth certificates, preneed funeral and burial plans. It is also helpful to have a list of contact numbers: physicians, insurance agents, attorneys, accountants, dentists, and clergy. You may want to keep photocopies of these in a "to be opened in case of emergency" envelope with certain relatives.

24. Questions about Holidays and Special Days

"Sometimes, through tears, the grieving must say as sad
a goodbye to traditions as they have to the people
with whom they have shared those traditions."
—*Harold Ivan Smith*[1]

"I hardly paid attention to what was going on until Anne
and Hannah hollered that they had the tree. It was the
scrawniest, most twisted tree on the lot, an ugly duckling
of a tree, and one my daughters explained that this year we
should give a home to the ugliest Christmas tree we could
find. We could love, celebrate and decorate this tree, which
no one else would ever choose."
—*Donald L. Murray*[2]

Q147 What about Christmas? My husband loved Christmas. He always wanted the biggest tree he could find and lit up the outside of our house. What should I do this year?

Do what you *can*—not what you cannot. Overlook the English
of the sentence; it's the reality many grievers find helpful. You
have permission to do Christmas "lite" this year.

Three holiday patterns are typical:

- *Holiday numb*—grievers are too numb to do anything
- *Holiday angry*—even grievers who may have been numb their first holiday season and received lots of support may be angry this holiday season because support has dwindled
- *Holiday go-for-it*—grievers who tackle the holidays "*fool* speed ahead" (that is not a typo)

It is difficult to go through the holidays when everyone else is celebrating and "making merry." Here are some practical suggestions. Sit down with a pad of paper and a pen and ponder:

- What is important about these holidays?
- What is not important?
- What is negotiable?

In making changes, you may want to consider these tips:

- *Prioritize*. Reflect on this seasonal question, "What is it that I need from *this* season?" Grant yourself freedom from the tyranny of the oughts, shoulds, and have tos that motivate the holidays.
- *Cut back*. Think about what is manageable emotionally. You may have shared the responsibilities of sending Christmas cards. You may have developed a system: one signs, one addresses. Every card can be a pounding reminder of the loss. Remember, the world is not going to fall apart if you do not send holiday cards this year. You may look over your list and limit it. Should you send the cards to individuals who may not know about the death? Should you send cards to your spouse's friends—some of whom you do not really know?
- *Innovate*. Even if Martha Stewart is a member of your family, don't feel pressured to decorate "as normal." Do what you can. Some grievers put up a tree but do not decorate it. Others decorate it only with lights. If a friend asks whether she can help, consider having her decorate the tree.

- *Redeem some support "coupons."* Remember those promises made at the funeral home? You may need to say, "I need help getting a Christmas tree. Could you help me do that?" Be specific. Be reasonable.
- *Recruit a "mall buddy."* If you need to shop, ask a friend to go along with you as your personal "mall buddy." Malls, with all the sights and sounds and smells of the holidays, can be overwhelming to grievers. A mall buddy can help you expedite your gift buying.
- *Give gift certificates.* One woman experiencing her first Christmas alone told me, "I could not face the buying, and the wrapping, and the mailing, and all that. Not this year. My husband was always the best helper." Instead, she ordered gift certificates for everyone on her list. She later told me that not one person complained about the gift certificates.

Sluggish Christmas sales are not your responsibility. Your responsibility is to grieve.

- *Limit gift giving.* Consider buying presents only for the children. Some families decide to contribute to the charity originally chosen for memorial gifts.
- *Watch the calories and seasonal numb-ers.* It is tempting in the "making of merry" to douse or dull our grief with food or drink. Some grievers cannot touch a thing during the holidays; others, graze through buffets, open houses, parties, etc. If you do the latter and gain weight, January will be very difficult. For some, the temptation is liquor. Or getting away and doing something exciting. Decisions have consequences.
- *Be mindful.* Christmas is a time to "be with" our grief. If you try to Scrooge your way through the holidays

unleashing your best imitation of "Bah, Humbug!" on others (remember, the root issue of Mr. Scrooge, if you read Dickens closely, was his unresolved grief), your cognitive dissonance and discomfort will only increase.

- *Give yourself permission to grieve out loud.* Lady Bird Johnson, First Lady, 1963–1969, lost her mother as a five-year-old. She offers freeing words you need to remind yourself of during the holidays, "Everybody needs an opportunity to hurt out loud."[1]
- *Take breathers from the season.* Remember the words of one wise griever: "This too will pass." However, if you do a "fool speed ahead" Christmas, you could get socked with a January depression of epic proportions.

Q148 On my child's first birthday after her death, I made a birthday cake. My husband, children, and I sat around the table and told stories, and my youngest child blew out the candles. When my father saw the pictures, he went ballistic, shouting "You've got to move on!" Isn't it still my daughter's birthday even if she isn't here to celebrate it?

Too bad your dad couldn't have tried that line on President Dwight D. Eisenhower and received the general's response. After the death of his son, Ikky, in 1921, the president sent a dozen yellow long-stemmed roses to Mamie every year on Ikky's birthday, because yellow was Ikky's favorite color. It helped him acknowledge it was his son's birthday.[1]

In reality, most family members know it is your daughter's birthday. So why not just get it out in the open and creatively respond to it? I have sometimes e-mailed individuals after a death and on the deceased's birthday, "Wonder how they celebrate birthdays in heaven?" Some, admittedly, were a little surprised initially, but as they thought about the question, they liked it.

Alan Wolfelt has comforted—and permissioned—many grievers with these words: "Remembering the person I have loved does allow me to heal slowly. Healing does not mean I forget. Actually, it means I will remember."[2]

Jesus said we should celebrate the Eucharist "in remembrance of me" (1 Corinthians 11:25). Feel free to celebrate your daughter's birthday in whatever way makes you comfortable.

Q149 Every year around the anniversary of our son's death, my wife becomes depressed. What can I do to help her?

Lots of individuals find anniversaries difficult. Christopher Andersen describes Caroline Kennedy Schlossberg's reaction to the anniversary of her brother's and sister-in-law's deaths: "Caroline handled it the way she had every other anniversary of a family death—by trying hard to ignore it. The Schlossbergs did nothing to mark the day and in fact tried to keep the children from reading about it or watching coverage on television."[1]

You may, however, want to borrow from a Jewish tradition that acknowledges the anniversary of a death with a *yahrzeit* ceremony. Mourners burn a twenty-four-hour candle leading up to the anniversary. Some go to a synagogue or temple and recite a prayer.

A *yahrzeit* ceremony gives you official permission to observe the anniversary of a death. If this is appealing to you, whether you are Jewish or not, I would encourage you to find a Jewish religious supply store and purchase a memorial candle (the ones I use are in metal, burn for twenty-six hours, and cost less than a dollar). Individuals who worry about "leaving a candle burning" may place the candle in water in the kitchen sink.

In the middle ages, people had "minning" days—they *reminded* themselves of loved ones who have died. Here are other suggestions for creating your own "minning" day:

- ↝ Buy a candle that represents colors your loved one liked.
- ↝ Place a memoriam in your local newspaper. One benefit

of this is that it encourages others to run a memoriam on their loved one's anniversary date.

- Do something that reminds you of your loved one. Play a favorite song. Request a favorite song on a radio station. Go to a favorite restaurant or "spot."

I hope you decide to honor the anniversary openly rather than in a stealthy manner. Give yourself permission to honor the anniversary. Sing along with Bob Hope, "Thanks for the Memories."

Q150 My friends tell me that birthdays and anniversaries are "for the living" not the dead! Is it alright to celebrate these special days?

Nothing alters the fact that this is the day your loved one was born or died or married you or married someone. Even the passing years cannot diminish the importance of the person to you. My friend Nancy e-mailed me this comment on the ninth anniversary of her brother John's death:

> I did manage some quiet time for me and John's memories last evening. . . . I still have a headache this morning from crying last night. I "STILL" miss him! Not a day goes by that I don't think of him. He was a great guy. Nine years have gone by and it still seems like yesterday.[1]

You may decide to celebrate quietly by writing in a journal, looking through photos or videos, being reminded of this individual. If you listen to public radio, sponsor a particular broadcast or a day of programming on the anniversary or on your loved one's birthday. Or borrow a practice from President Chester Arthur, who was a widower. Every day he resided in the White House, he placed fresh flowers in front of photos of his deceased wife, Ellen.[2] If a president can do it, you can do it.

If someone criticizes you—or says something that sounds like criticism to you—remind him or her that you are honoring

25. Questions about Finding Help

your loved one in a meaningful way.

> "Different individuals grieve in different ways,
> and counsellors [sic] should be aware
> of the diversity of such ways if they are
> to assist clients to follow their path of grief."
> —*Tony Walter*[1]

Q151 How do I find a counselor who understands my grief?

Not everyone who hangs up a shingle is grief-competent. A significant number of professional counselors and therapists—even those with PhDs or MSs—are *not* griever-friendly. They may be mourning-friendly for a particular

Referrals are significant in leading you to a "good" counselor.

period of time, but they may have some magical time sequence in their counseling. Some label pathological any griever who keeps their grief beyond a set period of time. Remember there is little in doctoral preparation in counseling on grief. (Why should there be? The goal is to get them over it!) Despite the grief resulting from 2.3 million deaths each year in the United States, there is no accredited PhD program in thanatology (death, dying, and bereaving), although there are some master's level programs.

Of course there are grief-experienced counselors who become professional companions to clients in grief. Many belong to the Association for Death Education and Counseling and have received the recognition, Certified in Thanatology. Look for a counselor in your community who holds this certification.

Ask your funeral director for referrals. Contact the bereavement specialist at your local hospice, or talk to the chaplain in the spiritual wellness office of your local hospital. Ministers, these days, do less grief counseling because of the pace of their ministries (or their own discomfort with grief issues). Most know individuals to whom they can make a confident referral. Ask directors of your company's Employee Assistance Program.

In your first meeting with a prospective counselor, feel free to interview the candidate. Ask about personal attitudes on grief. Ask about experiences working with individuals going through your particular type of loss. If the counselor talks about stages of grief, or implies a "move-on-and-get-over-it" attitude, move on to another professional relationship. Remember, counseling is an investment in you and in your future.

Q152 Do grief groups help?

The question is: Help you do or achieve what? A group is influenced by its leaders or facilitators' training and perspectives on grief. Some groups, unfortunately, aim to get you over the grief or to "fix" you. I heard about a group that advertises, "from grief to joy in fifteen weeks."

Instead, look for groups that offer safe places where you can talk about your grief and learn from other grievers. Great grief groups offer *mekom hanekhama*—safe places of comfort. In my book *Death and Grief*, I wrote:

> A support group is a healthy, safe place for you who are grieving to bring yourselves, your stories, your anger, and your bewilderment, and to know that it's just likely that others will have been there and recognize in your story parts of their story. And it is possible that something in your story will encourage another griever in the group.[1]

There are many types of groups out there. Some groups develop an ongoing approach, meeting weekly or monthly.

Other groups are time-focused. Unfortunately, there has been a growth of the *videologue* approach in which grievers passively watch a video and then talk about it.

As an individual who has facilitated Grief Gatherings in a medical center for years and written three books on grief groups, I consider *mutual help* support groups a wise investment in one's future. I prefer mutual help groups because the focus is not on the leader's credentials but on what each member contributes to the group. In mutual help groups, participants learn from each other.

Wonderful things happen in groups—sometimes when you least expect it. At the conclusion of the first session of groups I lead at Saint Luke's Hospital, participants stand in a circle and look at each other. I say, "You are standing in a circle with some of the most courageous individuals I know. They know things that you need to know. If you choose not to come back, someone will miss the lesson you could teach."

Q153 I have tried widows' support groups. There were widows who had been coming to the group for years! I went home more depressed than before the meeting. How do I find a healthy group?

There are groups, unfortunately, that encourage a "poor us" mentality, focusing on the past rather than the future. For some individuals, a group is the only place they go to seek comfort and assistance. Some of the best recruiters for our groups at Saint Luke's are those who attended other groups, participated in a Grief Gathering, and know the difference.

Ask participants of other groups, "Did (does) this help you? Was your grief honored or diminished?" Harold Kushner was not a renowned author on death the first time he walked into a meeting of The Compassionate Friends—he was a grieving parent. Years later, he reflected on his experience:

> It was a lifeline for us when we needed it, and we remain grateful for its help. . . . We discovered how important it was to be with people who understood our emotional need to tell the story over and over when our friends were telling us "get over it and get on with your life" and we discovered how helpful we could be to other bereaved parents by telling them that we had the same fantasies and the same guilt feelings they did.

Kushner noted that he and his wife "attended for three or fourth months and then 'graduated.'"[1]

Q154 My husband asks, "What good will it do to go to a counselor?" Should I go alone?

Sometimes, a griever has to do what a griever has to do. Admittedly, grief counseling would work better in tandem, but if your spouse will not go, or will not cooperate enthusiastically with the counseling, go it alone. In time, your spouse may come around.

Good counseling is about vulnerability and acknowledging the real relationship with the deceased as well as sources of conflict between co-survivors. Your husband may be afraid where some of those discussions could go.

Go. It will do you good. In some cases, there is a splash effect. Some insight you learn you will be able to pass on to other family members or friends.

Q155 The funeral home offers an aftercare program. What is it? Should I take advantage of it?

"Aftercare" is an umbrella term that covers a variety of approaches to providing continuing care for grieving clients after the funeral.

Ask about the qualifications and experience of the leader. Some facilitators are well-trained in group dynamics but not in grief. The ideal leader is sensitive with grievers and has a graduate degree, training in bereavement studies, and the Certified in Thanatalogy designation.

Be cautious about the individual who leads aftercare programs or groups whose experience is primarily personal. While their experience of loss, say an adolescent son's death, is their experience, what they have learned may not be transferable to other losses.

If aftercare sounds anything like, "Listen up!" or "Here are the one, two, threes of grief recovery" or a rehash of the stages of grief, this aftercare program will not be a safe place for you to do grief work. You want a leader who respects *your* individual grief experience. Grief care does not come in a "one size fits all" program.

Aftercare is offered as a free service, or at nominal rates, by many funeral homes that want to demonstrate, "We are concerned about your grieving as we were about your mourning."

Q156 Are internet "chat rooms" helpful for grievers?

Internet "chat rooms" are a part of the landscape. Some individuals have found chat rooms to be helpful, something of a safe place to face grief. For individuals in isolated communities or who do not have insurance coverage for counseling, chat rooms may be a helpful transitional response. Dennis Apple, a grief specialist, notes, "I think they are helpful but are still second-best to a support group or to a one-on-one meeting with someone who is very 'present.'" Apple also believes the chat room can be helpful to individuals between meetings.[1]

Clearly, not all chat rooms are safe spaces. My first experience with a chat room was immediately following the death of Princess Diana. I was stunned that there were individuals from all over the world in the room, and I was surprised by the depth of emotion being expressed. However, I was dumbfounded when one message appeared: "Ding! Dong! The Bitch is dead! And aren't we glad!" This verbal hand grenade was devastating to some in the room.

Having expressed some degree of tolerance for this Internet innovation, I want to caution that a chat room can become harmful if it prevents or diminishes conversation with family and friends. Some grievers will find it easier, perhaps too easy, to talk to a complete stranger in cyberland than to a friend or family member or spouse. However, the long-term health of family relationships necessitates communication about the death *within* the family.

Secondly, the conversation in a chat room can become too intimate. The feeling that "I can tell him/her anything" sometimes move the chats beyond grief. "He understands me!" can be a delicious but dangerous conclusion. There are individuals in chat rooms who take advantage of vulnerable, needy, grieving individuals. Many victims are too embarrassed about being taken in by an opportunist to talk about it.

It is essential that a griever acknowledge how much time is spent in chat rooms—perhaps by keeping a log. If the individual is "hiding" the chat room experience from others, that is a sign of potential trouble.

Make sure your physician knows all the prescriptions you are taking.

Q157 My physician wants to give me an antidepressant that he says "will help me." Should I take this? For how long?

Given the dominance of the "medical" perception of grief and the HMO-ization of health care, physicians rarely have time listen to grief narratives. At least in managed care structures, the average physician-patient encounter is about eight minutes.[1] How can a woman married fifty-four years or a mother of a dead six-year-old "explain" her grief experience to a physician in eight, or eighteen, minutes? Too many busy physicians reach for a prescription pad and mumble something about how "this will help you," or they refer the patient to a therapist.

Admittedly, some grievers can be helped by a good night's sleep—or a series of good sleeps. Yet many grief counselors are concerned about the *pharmacolization* of grief, whether antidepressants or sleeping pills or both. Victor Parachin cautions, "Prescription drugs and other numbing agents, such as alcohol, should be avoided. Sooner or later, your body will take over and allow you to rest properly."[2]

A medicated approach has many risks. Given the number of physicians a particular griever may be seeing—and the danger that each doctor may be unaware of what others are prescribing—the griever could accidentally be overmedicated. Or in the fog of grief, a griever may forget to take medications or take the medication twice. Some grievers turn to alcohol to dull the pain, and they may forget that alcohol should not be consumed while taking certain prescriptions.

Historically, pharmacists often "caught" prescription overlaps. Today, individuals may have certain prescriptions filled at a particular pharmacy in order to save money, or order it on the Internet. Others may obtain medications from well-meaning friends. Thus some hurting individuals fall through the supervisory window. They become medical time bombs waiting to go off.

Conclusion

"Questions are disturbing, especially those which may
threaten our traditions, our institutions, our security.
But questions never threaten the living God."
—*Madeleine L'Engle*[1]

I might never have written this book if I had not had Robert
Shea for world history class at Butler High School in Shively,
Kentucky. The first day of class, and periodically thereafter (particularly on days before tests), he stated with the intensity of a
marine drill sergeant, "There is no such thing as a stupid question. The only 'stupid question' is the unasked question!"

I might never have written this book had Dean Leland
Hughes, every Thursday morning at the Kentucky School of
Mortuary Science, not barged into our classroom demanding,
"And what questions do you wish to ask?"

Two teachers taught me the importance of asking questions
and weighing answers to questions.

Grievers Ask was never intended to be the "complete" book
of questions on grief. It is a beginning point. It reflects the

author's belief that over time—in some cases, eternal time—question marks become periods. I am hoping that you, at least, do not feel as alone as when you began reading and that in your reading you have found a seedling of hope.

I also hope you have shared this book—or some of the questions and answers—with other family, friends, individuals in your grief support group, or your counselor.

Rabbi David Wolpe hit a bull's-eye with his observation, "Sooner or later every one of us becomes an expert on grief."[2] I am not an expert, but one who has listened to lots of grievers.

Grief is the price we pay for relationships. I suppose hermits who live on islands, in caves, or deep in the woods, in the absence of relationships, do not grieve. Or perhaps unasked, unanswerable questions about grief sent them to that lonely place.

One final suggestion: Be gentle with your questions. Give your questions a voice.

Appendix A: Grief Resources

C. S. Lewis, as portrayed in the movie *Shadowlands,* observes, "We read to know that we are not alone." Many grievers read, particularly those who do not feel free talking about their grief. Reading challenges the sense of loneliness and isolation many grievers experience. This reading is classified as bibliotherapy. Some individuals have expressed, "I read everything I can get my hands on." I have been stunned to see their books underlined and marked up, spines broken. The books have coffee stains and tear stains. Often, they have been passed from one griever to another.

Many grievers find a first-person, "advice from the trail" type of book more helpful than the "how to grieve" resources. There are many personal experience books on the market. Unfortunately, very few are read by thanatologists before publication. Some readers assume that if it is in "black and white," it's gospel. Keep in mind that what worked for one griever may not work for you. Read cautiously.

Ask a librarian, funeral director, support group facilitator, counselor, or minister for guidance in reading selections. While flowers have been a traditional way to express condolences, some individuals prefer to give a good book or books, even knowing the books will not be read initially. Books, like some medications, are "time-released."

General Death

Attig, Thomas. (2000). *The Heart of Grief: Death and the Search for Lasting Love.* New York: Oxford University Press. Although many grieving individuals think they have to give up their love, Attig helps readers finds ways to love "in the absence."

Bartocci, Barbara. (2002). *From Hurting to Happy: Transforming Your Life after Loss.* Notre Dame, Ind.: Sorin Books. Bartocci helps readers understand that all major loss is understood incrementally.

Elison, Jennifer, and McGonigle, Chris. (2003). *Liberating Losses: When Death Brings Relief.* New York: Perseus Publishing. These wise authors give readers permission to acknowledge that not every deceased is a "loved one." Sometimes, grief is a relief.

Lewis, C. S. (1961). *A Grief Observed.* New York: Bantam. This classic contains the observations of the noted writer following the death of his wife, Joy. Millions have found this short book a comforting companion for the journey.

Lynch, Thomas. (1997). *The Undertaking: Life Studies from the Dismal Trade.* New York: Norton. From a long career of helping bury the dead and comfort the mourning, Lynch offers wisdom for this journey called grief.

Manning, Doug. (1979). *Don't Take My Grief Away.* San Francisco: Harper & Row. Few books match the title so accurately. Manning is clear: Do not let anyone take your grief away from you.

Parachin, Victor M. (2001). *Healing Grief.* St. Louis: Chalice Press. This griever-friendly title is a wonderful companion for those early days of grief and for moments when we want to revisit our grief.

Roberts, Barbara K. (2002). *Death without Denial, Grief without Apology: A Guide for Facing Death and Loss.* Troutdale, Ore.: NewSage Press. Roberts, widowed as governor of Oregon, believes that life "is too precious and grieving too important" to turn it into a closeted experience.

Wolpe, David. (1999). *Making Loss Matter: Creating Meaning in Difficult Times.* New York: Riverhead Books. Rabbi Wolpe helps individuals answer the question, "How can I make this loss meaningful?"

Death of a Child

Gamino, Louis A. and Cooney, Ann Taylor. (2002). *When Your Baby Dies through Miscarriage or Stillbirth*. Minneapolis: Augsburg Books. A couple's pilgrimage through grief offers practical insights into perinatal loss.

Huntley, Theresa. (2001). *When Your Child Loses a Loved One*. Minneapolis: Augsburg Books. Wise advice for your child's first significant death experience.

Huntley, Theresa. (1991). *When Your Child Dies*. Minneapolis: Augsburg Books. The death of a child is life's greatest outrage. Huntley offers wisdom to those who must walk this grief path.

Vogel, Susan Sonnenday. (2003). *And Then Mark Died: Letters of Grief, Love, & Faith*. Nashville: Abingdon. Losing a child is a parent's worst nightmare, regardless of the age of the son or daughter. Through letters, readers find insight in the experience of one grieving mother.

Waltman, Dawn Siegrist. (2002). *In a Heartbeat: A Journey of Hope and Healing for Those Who Have Lost a Baby*. Colorado Springs: Faithful Woman/Cook Communications. Waltman enfranchises grief for stillborns in this wonderful griever-friendly book.

Weems, Ann. (1995). *Psalms of Lament*. Louisville, Ky.: Westminster John Knox Press. Weems' son died on his twenty-first birthday. In her angst, she turned to the psalms and rewrote several dozen to voice her lament.

Death of a Parent

Bartocci, Barbara. (2000). *Nobody's Child Anymore: Grieving, Caring, and Comforting When Parents Die*. Notre Dame, Ind.: Sorin Press. One of the major responsibilities of adulthood, for many, is burying a parent. Bartocci offers wise guidance on the "ups and downs" of this experience.

Gilbert, Richard. (1999). *Finding Your Way after Your Parent Dies*. Notre Dame, Ind.: Ava Maria Press. Gilbert helps adult parent grievers examine feelings that are distinctly unique.

Smith, Harold Ivan. (2003). *Grieving the Death of a Mother*. Minneapolis: Augsburg Books. This book is a guide for individuals wandering an emotional landscape for which Fodor has no resource.

Smith, Harold Ivan. (1995). *On Grieving the Death of a Father*.

Minneapolis: Augsburg Books. The death of a father can be one of life's significant defining moments. Smith offers insights from some sixty historical personalities and celebrities.

Grief during the Holidays

Smith, Harold Ivan. (1999). *A Decembered Grief: Living with Loss When Others Are Celebrating*. Kansas City, Mo.: Beacon Hill Press. The holidays can be brutal for grievers. This resource offers practical ways to deal with the holidays.

Smith, Harold Ivan. (2001). *Journaling Your Decembered Grief*. Kansas City, Mo.: Beacon Hill Press. This companion to *A Decembered Grief* provides space to respond to the author's questions and observations.

Death of a Grandchild

Reed, Mary Lou. (2000). *Grandparents Cry Twice*. Amityville, N. Y.: Baywood. Grandparents grieve twice: for the child and for their son or daughter. Too many get lost in the "I have to be strong" mode.

Death of a Friend

Smith, Harold Ivan. (1996). *Grieving the Death of a Friend*. Minneapolis: Augsburg Books. One significant disenfranchised grief is for friends, who encounter the reaction, "It's not like they were family." The author examines the grief of dozens of historical personalities who lost a friend.

Smith, Harold Ivan. (2002). *When Your Friend Dies*. Minneapolis: Augsburg Books. This short easy-read book acknowledges that friends' grief counts.

Death of a Pet

Carmack, Betty J. (2002). *Grieving the Death of a Pet*. Minneapolis: Augsburg Books. Pet owners know it was "more than a pet" yet the culture wants to say that this grief does not count. Carmack's book is a valuable resource for those grieving a pet's death.

Rylant, Cynthia. (1995). *Dog Heaven*. New York: Blue Sky Press. In a children's book format, Rylant dances with the question, "Do dogs go to heaven?"

Rylant, Cynthia. (1997). *Cat Heaven.* New York: Blue Sky Press. This is a wonderful resource for individuals who have had a cat die.

Widowhood

Greene, Phyllis. *Shedding Years.* New York: Villard. Wise words from a widow who has "been there."

Suicide

Grollman, Earl A., and Malikow, Max. (1999). *Living When a Young Friend Commits Suicide.* Boston: Beacon Press. A straightforward resource about suicide that gives comfort and expert ideas for helping yourself.

Children and Grief

Fitzgerald, Helen. (1992). *The Grieving Child: A Parent's Guide.* New York: Fireside Books. A practical resource to provide invaluable suggestions for helping a child "deal" with grief.

Grief and Counseling

Worden, J. William. (2002). *Grief Counseling and Grief Therapy: A Handbook for the Mental Health Practitioner.* (3rd ed.). New York: Springer. This is the definitive resource for grief counseling.

Appendix B:
Prayer Resources

Archdiocese of Chicago. (1995). *Prayers for Those Who Mourn.* Chicago, Ill.: Liturgy Training Publications.

Hamilton, Lisa Belcher. (2001). *For those We Love But No Longer See: Daily Offices for Times of Grief.* Brewster, Mass.: Paraclete Press.

Harcourt, Giles, and Harcourt, Melville. (1978). *Short Prayers for the Long Day.* Liguori, Mo.: Trumph Books.

Oman, Maggie (ed.). (1997). *Prayers for Healing: 365 Blessings, Poems, & Meditations from around the World.* Berkeley, Calif.: Conari Press.

Peale, Norman Vincent. (1993). *My Favorite Prayers.* San Francisco: HarperSanFrancisco.

Roberts, Elizabeth, and Amidon, Elias. (1996). *Life Prayers from around the World: 365 Prayers, Blessings, and Affirmations to Celebrate the Human Journey.* San Francisco: HarperSanFrancisco.

Schiller, David (ed.). (1996). *The Little Book of Prayers.* New York: Workman Publishing.

Washington, James Melvin (ed.). (1994). *Conversations with God: Two Centuries of Prayers by African Americans.* New York: HarperCollins.

Notes

Introduction

1. Dick Gilbert, *Finding Your Way after Your Parent Dies* (Notre Dame, Ind.: Ava Maria Press, 1999), 62.
2. Doug Manning, *Don't Take My Grief Away: What to Do When You Lose a Loved One* (San Francisco: Harper & Row, 1979), 47.
3. Robert Sobel, *Coolidge: An American Enigma* (Washington, D. C.: Regnery, 1998), 297.
4. Dave Dravecky, Jan Dravecky, with Ken Gire, *When You Can't Come Back: A Story of Courage and Grace* (Grand Rapids, Mich.: Zondervan, 1991), 144.

Chapter 1: Questions about the Duration of Grief

1. Ellen Goodman, "Mourning Gets the Bum's Rush," *The Kansas City Star*, 2 August 1998, B7.
2. Alan D. Wolfelt, lecture, Olathe, Kansas, 17 February 1999.
3. Carol Fredericks Ebeling, *What to Say: 52 Positive Ways to Show Christian Sympathy to Those Who Grieve* (St. Louis, Mo.: Concordia, 2002), 59.
1:1. J. William Worden, *Grief Counseling and Grief Therapy: A Handbook for the Mental Health Practitioner,* 2nd edition (New York: Springer, 1991), 18.
1:2. Ebeling, *What to Say,* 25-26.
1:3. Richard Obershaw, "Myths of Grief," presentation at the National Funeral Director's Convention, Las Vegas, Nevada, 19 October 2003.
3:1. Stephen Ambrose, *Eisenhower: Soldier and President* (New York: Simon and Schuster, 1990), 38.
4:1. Harold S. Kushner, *The Lord Is My Shepherd: The Healing Wisdom of the Twenty-Third Psalm* (New York: Knopf, 2003), 98.
4:2. Rick Hampson and Martha T. Moore, "Two Years after Sept. 11, NYC

Couple to Bury Son: Closure Is Elusive for Many," *USA Today*, 4 September 2003, 1A.

5:1. Robert A. Neimeyer, *Lessons of Loss: A Guide to Caring* (New York: McGraw-Hill: Premis Custom Printing, 1998), 84.

5:2. Ibid., 83.

6:1. Goodman, "Mourning Gets the Bum's Rush," B7.

7:1. Worden, *Grief Counseling and Grief Therapy*, 3rd edition, 47.

7:2. Gordon Walker, *Dealing with Grief* (Ben Lomond, Calif.: Concilar Press, 1985), 7.

7:3. Tony Walter, "A New Model of Grief: Bereavement and Biography," *Mortality* 1(1) (1996), 20.

7:4. Hampson and Moore, "Two Years after Sept. 11," 2A.

8:1. Eric Schlosser, "A Grief Like No Other," *Atlantic Monthly*, September 1997, 50.

9:1. S. Bruce Vaughn, "Recovering Grief in the Age of Recovery," *The Journal of Pastoral Theology* 13:1 (2003), 40.

9:2. Ibid.

10:1. David Goldstein, "Carnahan Thanks Colleagues for Support in Farewell Address," *The Kansas City Star*, 19 November 2002, A4.

Chapter 2: Questions about Asking Why

1. Reynolds Price, *Letters to a Man in a Fire: Does God Exist and Does He Care?* (New York: Scribner, 1999), 63-64.

2. George H. Bush, *All the Best: My Life in Letters and Other Writings* (New York: Scribner, 1999), 592.

11:1. Richard Shenkman, *Presidential Ambition: How the Presidents Gained Power, Kept Power, and Got Things Done* (New York: Harper Collins, 1999), 92.

11:2. Michael Beschloss, *The American Heritage Illustrated History of the Presidents* (New York: Crown Publishers, 2000).

11:3. Frederica Mathewes-Green, *At the Corner of East and Now* (New York: Jeremy T. Tarcher, 1999), 57.

11:4. Joseph Scriven, "What a Friend We Have in Jesus," in Bert Polman, Marilyn Kay Stulken, and James Rawlings Sydnor, *Amazing Grace: Hymn Texts for Devotional Use* (Louisville, Ky.: Westminster John Knox Press, 1994), 233.

13:1. Ben Bradlee, *A Good Life: Newspapering and Other Adventures* (New York: Simon and Schuster, 1995), 262.

13:2. Christopher Andersen, *Jackie after Jack* (New York: William Morrow, 1998), 91.

Chapter 3: Questions about Remembering

1. Elizabeth Harper Neeld, *Seven Choices: Taking the Steps to a New Life after Losing Someone You Love* (New York: Delta/Dell, 1990), 226.

2. Thomas Attig, *The Heart of Grief: Death and the Search for Lasting Love* (New York: Oxford University Press, 2000), 23.

3. Nancy Cobb, *In Lieu of Flowers: A Conversation for the Living* (New York: Pantheon, 2000), 53.

14:1. Attig, *The Heart of Grief*, 27.

14:2. Walter, "A New Model of Grief," 14.

14:3. Harold Ivan Smith.

15:1. Ebeling, *What to Say*, 52

15:2. Dennis Klass, Phyllis R. Silverman, and Steven L. Nickman, *Continuing Bonds: New Understandings of Grief* (Washington, D.C.: Francis and Taylor, 1966).

15:3. Kushner, *The Lord Is My Shepherd*, 97-98.

16:1. Terese Rando, "The Increased Prevalence of Complicated Mourning: The Onslaught Is Just Beginning," *Omega* 26:1 (1992-93), 45.

16:2. Jennifer Elison and Chris McGonigle, *Liberating Losses: When Death Brings Relief* (New York: Perseus Publishing, 2003).

16:3. Denman Dewey III, "When a Congregation Cares: Organizing Ministry to the Bereaved," *Death Studies* 12:2 (1988), 123-135.

Chapter 4: Questions about Regrets

1. Attig, *The Heart of Grief*, 115.

18:1. *The Book of Common Prayer and Administration of the Sacraments and Other Rites and Ceremonies of the Church* (New York: Seabury, 1979), 323.

18:2. Harold Ivan Smith.

19:1. Ancient Persian prayer in *The Oxford Book of Prayer* (Oxford: Oxford University Press, 1985), 333.

Chapter 5: Questions about Causation

1. Charles A. Corr, Clyde M. Nabe, and Donna M. Corr, *Death and Dying, Life and Living*, 2nd edition (Pacific Grove, Calif.: Brooks/Cole, 1997), 41.

2. Ibid.

21:1. Adin Steinsaltz, *Simple Words: Thinking about What Really Matters in Life* (New York: Simon and Schuster, 1999), 161.

21:2. Alexandra Kathryn Mosca, *Grave Undertakings: Mortician by Day, Model by Night*, (Far Hills, N. J.: New Horizon Press, 2003), 210.

21:3. Dan Spaite, "Dealing with Grief 'Like a Christian': What the Bible Really Teaches," *Holiness Today*, September 2003, 10.

22:1. Dru Sefton, "Dissecting Autopsy: Myths Persist, But the Practice Can Benefit Survivors, Medical Community," *The Kansas City Star*, 7 April 1997, D5.

22:2. Richard K. Zarbo, Peter B. Baker, and Peter J. Howanitz, "The Autopsy As a Performance Measurement Tool-Diagnostic Discrepancies and Unresolved Clinical Questions," *Archives of Pathology Laboratory Medicine* 123 (1999), 192.

23:1. Steven Keyser, "Autopsy: A Fact of Life," *The Director,* August 2000, 36.

23:2. D. N. Saller, K. B. Lesser, U. Harrell, B. B. Rogers, and C. E. Oyer, "The Clinical Utility of Perinatal Autopsy," *The Journal of the American Medical Association* 273:8 (1995), 663.

22:3. Personal correspondence with Jay Harrison, MD, 11 September 2003.

Chapter 6: Questions about God

1. Peter J. Gomes, "Storm Center: When Bad Things Happen," *The Christian Century,* 31 May 2003, 10.

2. Marianne H. Micks, *Loving the Questions: The Exploration of the Nicene Creed* (Cambridge, Mass.: Cowley Press, 1993), 125.

25:1. Henry Sloane Coffin, "Alex's Death," in Phyllis Theroux (ed.), *The Book of Eulogies* (New York: Scribner, 1997), 747.

25:2. Kushner, *The Lord Is My Shepherd,* 107.

25:3. Ibid.

25:4. Ibid., 107-108.

25:5. Lewis Smedes, "What's God Up To? A Father Grieves the Loss of a Child," *The Christian Century,* 3 May 2003, 39.

26:1. Larry King with Rabbi Irwin Katsof, *Powerful Prayers* (Los Angeles: Renaissance, 1998), 35.

26:2. John H. Hewett, *After Suicide* (Louisville, Ky.: Westminister, 1980), 48.

26:3. David Van Biema, "When God Hides His Face," *Time,* 16 July 2001, 64.

27:1. C. Everett Koop and Elizabeth Koop, *Sometimes Mountains Move* (Wheaton, Ill.: Tyndale House, 1979), 93.

27:2. Victor Parachin, *Healing Grief* (St. Louis, Mo.: Chalice Press, 2001), 62.

27:3. Tr. Ernst W. Olson, © Board of Publication, Lutheran Church in America, admin. Augsburg Fortress.

28:1. Gilbert Meilaender, *Bioethics* (Grand Rapids, Mich.: Eerdmans, 1996), 60.

28:2. Diane Meier, "Many Doctors Lack Training to Ease Patients' Severe Pain," *USA Today,* 8 September 2003, 17A.

28:3. Kenneth L. Vaux and Sara A. Vaux, *Dying Well* (Nashville: Abingdon, 1996), 11.

28:4. Harold Ivan Smith, *Finding Your Way to Say Goodbye: Comfort for the Dying and Those Who Care for Them* (Notre Dame, Ind.: Ava Maria Press, 2002), 25.

30:1. Kenneth Kantzer, "Troublesome Questions," *Christianity Today,* 30 March 1987, 45.

30:2. Anne Graham Lotz, *Heaven: My Father's House* (Nashville: W Publishing Group, 2001), 108.

30:3. Pat Robertson, *Bring It On: Tough Questions, Candid Answers* (Nashville: W Publishing Group, 2003), 130.

30:4. Mike Anton and William Lobdell, "Belief in Hell," *The Kansas City Star,* 27 July 2002, G2.

31:1. Gomes, "Storm Center," 10.

Chapter 7: Questions about Grief and Spirituality

1. David J. Wolpe, *Making Loss Matter: Creating Meaning in Difficult Times,* (New York: Riverhead Books, 2000), 6.
2. Ibid.
3. Jack Morgan in Rob Zucker, Caring from the Heart: An Interview with Jack Morgan," *The Grief and Healing Newsletter,* Winter 2000, 3.
32:1. Worden, *Grief Counseling and Grief Therapy,* 1991, 14.
32:2. Peggy Benson, *Listening for a God Who Whispers: A Woman's Discovery of Quiet Understanding* (Nashville: Generoux, 1991), 153.
32:3. Christopher Andersen, *Sweet Caroline: Last Child of Camelot,* (New York: William Morrow, 2003), 303.
34:1. Vance Havner in Dan Zarda with Marcia Woodard [eds.], *Forever Remembered* (Seattle: Compendium, 1999), 54.
34:2. Lucinda Vardey [ed.], *Mother Teresa: A Simple Path* (New York: Ballentine, 1995), 7.
34:3. Donna Schaper, *Sacred Speech: A Practical Guide for Keeping Spirit in Your Speech* (Woodstock, Vt.: Skylights Paths Publishing, 2003), 44.
34:4. Paul Gerhardt, "Commit Thou All Thy Griefs," in Polman, Stilken, and Syndron (eds.), *Amazing Grace,* 44.
34:5. Isaac Watts, "O God, Our Help in Ages Past," in *The Lutheran Book of Worship,* 320.
34:6. Leo Rosten, *Leo Rosten's Treasury of Jewish Quotations* (New York: Bantam, 1977), 364.
35:1. Ed Dobson cited in Shelley, Marshall, Reed, Eric, Zahn, and Drew (eds.), "Leave room for God: Leadership Interview with Ed Dobson," *Leadership,* Fall 2001, 28.
35:2. Stephen E. Broyles, *The Wind That Destroys and Heals* (Colorado Springs: Shaw/Waterbrook Press, 2003).
35:3. Gracia Burnham with Dean Merrill, *In the Presence of My Enemies* (Wheaton, Ill.: Tyndale House, 2003).
35:4. John A. Peterson, "Dream of Burial at Arlington to Come 35 Years Late," *The Kansas City Star,* 29 May 2003, A4.
35:5. Robert J. Dufford, SJ and OCP Publications, © 1975, 1978. All rights reserved. Used with permission.

Chapter 8: Questions about Forgiveness

1. Gilbert, *Finding Your Way after Your Parent Dies,* 41.
38:1. www.madd/org/home, September 2003.
38:2. Janice Lord. "Really MAAD: Looking Back 20 Years." *Driven Magazine,* Spring 2000, as found on www.madd.org.
39:1. Smedes, "What's God Up To?" 38.
39:2. Ibid.
39:3. Ibid.
39:4. Ibid.
39:5. Ibid.

39:6. Ibid.

40:1. Gomes, "Storm Center."

42:1. Thomas Merton, *New Seeds of Contemplation* (Boston: Shambhala, 1961/2003), 57.

42:2. Scriven, "What a Friend We Have in Jesus."

Chapter 9: Questions about Eternal Life, Heaven, and Hell

1. Elizabeth A. Johnson, *Friends of God and Prophets* (New York: Continuum, 1999), 211.

43:1. Christine cited in Sue Howard and Gail Howard, *I Am Afraid* (Pasadena, Calif.: World-Wide Missions, 1973), 25.

43:2. C. S. Lewis quoted in Sherwood Eliot Wirt and Kersten Beckstrom, *Topical Encyclopedia of Living Quotations* (Minneapolis: Bethany House, 1982), 106.

44:1. Christopher Andersen, *The Day John Died* (New York: William Morrow, 2000), 73.

44:2. Ibid., 74.

45:1. C. S. Lewis, "Preface," in Dorothy Sayers, J. R. R. Tolkien, C. S. Lewis, A. O. Barfield, Gervase Mathew, and W. H. Lewis, *Essays Presented to Charles Williams* (Grand Rapids, Mich.: Eerdmans, 1946/1966), xiv.

45:2. Broyles, *The Wind That Destroys and Heals,* 27.

46:1. Maya Angelou, *Wouldn't Take Nothing for My Journey Now* (New York: Random House, 1993), 48.

46:2. Frederick William Faber, "There's a Wideness in God's Mercy," in *Amazing Grace,* 212.

47:1. Albert Y. Hsu, *Grieving a Suicide: A Loved One's Search for Comfort, Answers, and Hope* (Downer's Grove, Ill.: InterVarsity, 2002), 105.

47:2. Ibid., 106.

47:3. Ibid.

48:1. "Dr. Pierce Reveals in Sermon Two Incidents," *The Mercersburg News,* 21 November 1924, 8, courtesy Herbert Hoover Presidential Library.

50:1. Karl Rahner cited in William J. Elliott, *A Place at the Table* (New York: Doubleday, 2003), 91.

50:2. Gerald L. Zelizer, "Churches Give Hell a Makeover," *USA Today,* 21 February 2000, 15A.

51:1. Linda Tober and F. Stanley Lusby, "Heaven and Hell," in Mircea Eliode (ed.), *The Encyclopedia of Religion,* volume 6 (New York: Macmillian, 1986), 239.

51:2. Albert Truesdale, "Holy Love vs. Eternal Hell: The Wesleyan Options," *The Wesleyan Theological Journal* 36:1 (2001), 109.

51:3. Ibid.

51:4. Ibid., 111.

52:1. Morton Kelsey, *Afterlife: The Other Side of Dying* (New York: Paulist Press, 1979), 227.

52:2. S. Radhakkrishnan, *The Bhagavaddgita* (1948) cited in Corr, Nabe, and Corr, *Death and Dying,* 523.

52:3. Philip Ruge-Jones, *What Happens in the End? Basic Questions* (Minneapolis: Augsburg, 1998), 19.

52:4. David Ford, *Prayers and the Departed Saints* (Ben Lomond, Calif.: Concilar Press, 1991/1994), 12.

52:5. Kelsey, *Afterlife,* 236.

53:1. Corr, Nabe, and Corr, *Death and Dying,* 528.

53:2. R. H. Lifton cited in Ibid.

53:3. Ibid., 524.

53:4. John L. Esposito, *Islam: The Straight Path* (New York: Oxford University Press, 1998), 25.

53:5. Lynne DeSpelder and Albert Lee Strickland, *The Last Dance: Encountering Death and Dying,* 6th edition (Mountain View, Calif.: McGraw-Hill, 2002), 510.

53:6. Arthur O. Roberts, *Prayers at Twilight* (Newberg, Ore.: Barclay Press, 2003), 19, used with permission.

Chapter 10: Questions about Grief and Communication

1. "Shriver Book Explores Meaning of Death," *USA Today,* July 21, 1999.

54:1. Greg Orr, *The Blessing: The Memoir* (San Francisco: Council Oak Books, 2002).

57:1. Steinsaltz, *Simple Words,* 161.

58:1. Dexter King with Ralph Wiley, *Growing Up King: An Intimate Memoir* (New York: Warner, 2003), 61.

61:1. Theodore G. Tappert, Willem J. Kooiman, and Lowell C. Green, *The Mature Luther,* volume three (Decorah, Ia.: Luther College Press, 1959), 68.

61:2. Ibid.

61:3. Bush, *All the Best,* 51.

61:4. Ibid., 578.

61:5. Ibid., 443.

61:6. Andersen, *Sweet Caroline,* 253.

62:1. Therese Rando, *Parental Loss of a Child* (Champaign, Ill.: Research Press, 1986), 37.

62:2. Mary Lou Reed, "Grandparents' Grief–Who Is Listening?" *The Forum* (January-March, 2003), 3.

62:3. Mary Lou Reed, *Grandparents Cry Twice* (Amityville, N.Y.: Baywood, 2000).

62:4. "Grandparents Take Role in Parenting," *The Kansas City Star,* 19 October 2003, 19A.

63:1. Wolpe, *Making Loss Matter,* 5.

63:2. Neimeyer, *Lessons of Loss,* 46-47.

Chapter 11: Questions about the Death of a Parent

1. Gary Small cited in Barbara Bartocci, *Nobody's Child Anymore: Grieving, Caring, and Comforting When Parents Die* (Notre Dame, Ind.: Sorin Books, 2000), 41.
2. Darcie Sims cited in Dick Gilbert, *Finding Your Way after Your Parent Dies*, 12.
67:1. "Lonely Victims of Heat Silently Buried in Paris," *The Kansas City Star*, 4 September 2003, A8.

Chapter 12: Questions about the Death of a Child

1. Howard Twitty and Michael Arkush, "I'll Never Forget," *Sports Illustrated*, 25 April 2003, G9.
2. Barbara Bush, *Barbara Bush: A Memoir* (New York: Charles Scribner's Sons, 1994), 46.
3. Thomas Lynch, *The Undertaking: Life Studies from the Dismal Trade* (New York: Norton, 1997), 51.
68:1. Bush, *Barbara Bush*, 41.
68:2. Mark Hardt and Danette Carroll, "Divorce and the Death of a Child," *Bereavement*, (May/June, 1998), 6.
68:3. Ibid.
68:4. Shirley A. Murphy, L. Clark Johnson, and Janet Lohan, "Finding meaning in a Child's Violent Death: A Five-Year Prospective Analysis of Parents' Personal Narratives and Empirical Data," *Death Studies* 27, 2003, 381-404.
68:5. Dick Gilbert, personal correspondence, 10 October 2003.
68:6. Susan Eisenhower, *Mrs. Ike: Memories and Reflections on the Life of Mamie Eisenhower* (New York: Farrar, Straus, & Giroux, 1996), 73.
68:7. Carlo D'Este, *Eisenhower: A Soldier's Life* (New York: Henry Holt, 2002), 157.
68:8. Edward Klein, *The Kennedy Curse: Why Tragedy Has Haunted America's First Family for 150 Years* (New York: St. Martin's Press, 2003).
68:9. Christopher Andersen, *Jackie after Jack*, 88.
69:1. George W. Bush, *A Charge to Keep* (New York: William Morrow, 1999), 14.
69:2. Ibid.
69:3. Bush, *Barbara Bush*, 46.
69:4. Susan Sonnenday Vogel, *And Then Mark Died: Letters of Grief, Love, and Faith* (Nashville: Abingdon, 2003), 44.
70:1. Gerard Brender, *Martin Luther: Theology and Revolution* (New York: Oxford University Press, 1991), 344.
71:1. Dawn Siegrist Waltman, *In a Heartbeat: A Journey of Hope and Healing for Those Who Have Lost a Baby* (Colorado Springs: Faithful Woman/David C. Cook, 2002), 115.
71:2. Ibid.

72:1. Del Jones, "Burger King CEO Hopes to Help by Sharing His Grief," *USA Today,* 14 November 2001, 2B.

Chapter 13: Questions about Children and Grief

1. Neimeyer, *Lessons of Loss,* 42.
73:1. Bush, *A Charge to Keep,* 15.
73:2. Helen Fitzgerald, *The Grieving Child: A Parent's Guide* (New York: Fireside, 1991), 171.
74:1. James Robert Parish, *Rosie: Rosie O'Donnell's Biography* (New York: Carroll and Graft, 1997).
74:2. Christopher Andersen, *The Day John Died* (New York: William Morrow, 2000), 84.
75:1. Alan Wolfelt, "Helping Children Cope with Grief," (Batesville, Ind.: Batesville Management Services, 1992), 4.

Chapter 14: Questions about Suicide

1. Hewett, *After Suicide,* 51.
79:1. Centers for Disease Control, "National Center for Injury Prevention and Control," *Suicide in the United States,* 24 August 2003, 2-3. www.cdc.gov.ncipc/factsheets/suifacts.htm.
80:1. Ibid.
80:2. Centers for Disease Control, "Programs for the Prevention of Suicide among Adolescents and Young Adults," *Morbidity and Mortality Weekly Report* 43, 22 April 1994, 13.
80:3. Howard Schubiner, "How to Identify the Suicidal Teen," *Medical Aspects of Human Sexuality,* June 1991, 41.
80:4. "Young People with Suicide on their Minds," *USA Today,* 15 July 2002, 6D.
80:5. Gary Remafedi, James A. Fallow, and Robert W. Deischer, "Risk Factors for Attempted Suicide in Gay and Bisexual Youth," *Pediatrics* 87:6 (1999), 869.
80:6. Ibid., 871.
81:1. Michael Taylor, "Golden Gate Bridge's Fatal Attraction," *The San Francisco Chronicle,* 14 July 1995, A19.
81:2. Ibid.
81:3. Earl Grollman and Max Malikow, *Living When a Young Friend Commits Suicide* (Boston: Beacon Press, 1999), 18.
81:4. Mike Feinsilber, "Admiral Killed Self to Avoid Dishonoring Sailors," *West Hawaii Today,* 25 November 1996, 3A.
81:5. Corr, Nabe, and Corr, *Death and Dying,* 496.
82:1. Centers for Disease Control, http://.www.cdc.gov.ncipc/factsheets/suifacts.htm.
82:2. Dick Gilbert, personal correspondence, 10 October 2003.
82:3. Deborah Sharp, "Senior Suicides to Increase As U.S. Ages," 20 February 2003, *USA Today,* 3A.
82:4. Ibid.

83:1. DeSpelder and Strickland, *The Last Dance*, 449-450.

83:2. Ibid., 450.

83:3. Victor Parachin, "How to 'Suicide Proof' Your Teen," *Christian Educator*, September 2003, 22.

84:1. Centers for Disease Control, http://.www.cdc.gov.ncipc/factsheets/ suifacts.htm.

84:2. Elizabeth R. Woods, Yvonne G. Lin, Amy Middleman, Patricia Beckford, Louise Chase, and Robert H. DuRant, "The Association of Suicide Attempts in Adolescents," *Pediatrics*, 99:6 (1997), 791.

84:3. Centers for Disease Control, "Suicide Among Children, Adolescents, and Young Adults, United States, 1980-1992," *Morbidity and Mortality Weekly Report* 44:15 (1995), 290.

85:1. Fitzgerald, *The Grieving Child*, 61.

85:2. Ibid., 62.

85:3. Ibid.

85:4. Peter Fonda, *Don't Tell Dad* (New York: Hyperion, 1998), 45.

85:5. Linda Goldman, "Suicide: How Can We Talk to the Children?," *The Forum* (May/June, 2000), 7.

85:6. Ibid.

85:7. Ibid.

86:1. Hsu, *Grieving a Suicide*, 10.

86:2. Ibid., 13.

86:3. Grollman and Malikow, *Living When a Young Friend Commits Suicide*, 11.

86:4. Nancy Reuben Greenfield, "Suicide: We're Finding Ways to Deal with This Disturbing Trend," *The Dallas Morning News*, 16 November 1997, 6J.

86:5. John R. Jordan, "Is Suicide Bereavement Different," *The Forum* May/June 2000, 3.

86:6. Ibid.

86:7. Hsu, *Grieving a Suicide*, 106.

86:8. Erica Goode, "How Sharing Grieve Can Ease the Pain: A Conversation with Henry Seiden and Christopher Lukas," *U.S. News & World Report*, 30 January 1989, 80.

87:1. Dietrich Bonhoeffer, *Ethics*, Eberhard Bethge (ed.), (New York: Macmillian, 1955), 172.

87:2. Meilaender, *Bioethics*, 59.

Chapter 15: Questions about the Death of a Pet

1. Betty J. Carmack, *Grieving the Death of a Pet* (Minneapolis: Augsburg, 2003), 2-3.

2. Billy Graham, "Animals in Heaven? Bible Is Unclear," *The Kansas City Star*, 22 December 1995, E5.

88:1. Webb Garrison, *Strange Facts about Death* (Nashville: Abingdon, 1989), 193.

88:2. Carmack, *Grieving the Death of a Pet*, 6.

88:3. Pamela Kilian, *Barbara Bush: Matriarch of a Dynasty* (New York: Thomas Dunne Books/St. Martin's Press, 2002), 204.

89:1. Carmack, *Grieving the Death of a Pet*, 117.

89:2. Ibid., 118.

89:3. Billy Graham, "Heaven Might Include Pets," *The Kansas City Star*, 10 August 2001, E3.

Chapter 16: Questions about Grief and Sexuality

1. Rana K. Limbo and Sara Rich Wheeler, *When a Baby Dies: A Handbook for Healing and Helping.* (LaCrosse, Wisc.: Resolve through Sharing, 1986).

2. Carol Miller, *Nursing for Wellness in Older Adults: Theory and Practice*, 4th ed. (Philadelphia: Lippincott, Williams, & Watkins, 2004).

91:1. Limbo and Wheeler, 25.

91:2. Ibid.

91:3. Rebekah Wang-Cheng, www.healthlink.mcw.edu.

93:1. Arthur Cushman McGiffert, *Martin Luther: The Man and His Work* (New York: The Century Company, 1919), 304.

93:2. Leslie Schover, *Sexuality and Cancer: For the Man Who Has Cancer, and His Partner* (New York: American Cancer Society, 1988), 29.

95:1. Wang-Cheng, www.healthlink.mcw.edu.

101:1. McGiffert, *Martin Luther*, 304.

Chapter 17: Questions about Funeral Rituals and Customs

1. Lynch, *The Undertaking*, 80.

2. Harold Ivan Smith, *ABCs of Healthy Grieving* (Shawnee Mission, Kans.: Shawnee Mission Medical Center, 2001), 56.

3. Barbara K. Roberts, *Death without Denial, Grief without Apology: A Guide for Facing Death and Loss* (Troutdale, Ore.: NewSage Press, 2002), 78-79.

103:1. Willard Stern Randall, *George Washington: A Life* (New York: Henry Holt, 1997), 502.

104:1. Therese Rando, *Grief, Dying, and Death: Clinical Interventions for Caregivers* (Champaign, Ill.: Research Press, 1984), 180-189.

104:2. Doug Manning, *The Funeral: A Chance to Touch, a Chance to Serve, a Chance to Heal* (Oklahoma City: In-Sight Books, 2001), 27.

104:3. Rando, 183.

106:1. Thomas Lynch, "Q&A with Thomas Lynch," *The Director*, December 2002, 32.

107:1. Lynch, *The Undertaking*, 197.

109:1. Elizabeth L. Post, *Emily Post's Etiquette*, 15th edition (New York: HarperCollins, 1992), 549.

111:1. David Cole, "Singing the Faith," *The Hymn* 51:3 (2000), 24.

111:2. David Tianen, "Baby Boomers Choosing Pop Music for Trip to the Great Beyond," *The Washington Post*, 24 February 2001, B9.

111:3. "Nontraditional Funeral Tunes: Rock, Country, Swing and Polka Highlight Today's Nontraditional Funerals," *The Director*, July 2001, 34-35.

112:1. Gerald L. Euster, "Memorial Contributions: Remembering the Elderly Deceased and Supporting the Bereaved," *Omega* 23:2 (1991), 169-179.

112:2. Bill Tammeus, "We Honor the Dead for Complex Reasons," *The Kansas City Star*, 23 August 2003, B7.

113:1. Carl Sterrazza Anthony, *Florence Harding: The First Lady, the Jazz Age, and the Death of America's Most Scandalous President* (New York: Quill, 1998), 473.

114:1. Victor Parachin, "Preaching at Funerals: A Guide for the Clergy," *The Director*, July 2003, 12.

115:1. Brent Russell, "Joseph of Arimathaea: The Patron Saint of Funeral Directors," *The Director*, October 1996, 56.

115:2. Todd Van Beck, "The Fossores: Our Early Funeral Directors and Cemeterians," *The Director*, March 2000, 60.

115:3. Davis Cressy, *Birth, Marriage, and Death: Ritual, Religion, and the Life-Cycle in Tudor and Stuart England* (New York: Oxford University Press, 1997), 429.

115:4. Lynch, *The Undertaking*, 181-182.

116:1. "Male/Female Enrollment," *The Director*, January 2003, 52.

116:2. Barbara LesStange, "An Interview with Kathy Ordiway," *The American Funeral Director*, September 2002, 122.

118:1. Susan Ager, "Your Wedding Day Your Way," *The Kansas City Star*, 3 August 2003, G1.

118:2. Manning, *The Funeral*, 22.

119:1. National Funeral Directors Association, "Average Profit Slipped to 7.63% in 2002," *The Director*, June 2003, 56.

119:2. Patricia Fripp cited in "Keeping Up with the Vigilante Consumer," *The American Funeral Director*, October 2003, 102.

120:1. Christine Dugas, "Prepaid Funerals Can Have Pitfalls: Check All Factors before Putting Funds into Final Resting Place," *USA Today*, 23 September 2003, 3B.

121:1. Ann Landers, "Been There in Chicago," *The Kansas City Star*, 6 July 1994, F6.

Chapter 18: Questions about Cremation

1. T. Scott Gilligan, "Liability after Cremation," *The Director*, August 1998, 43.

2. James P. Moroney, "Cremation and the Catholic Church," *The Director*, August 1998, 51.

122:1. "2002 U.S. Cremation Rate Projected to Reach 27.78%," *The American Funeral Director*, October 2003, 82.

124:1. Warren Duzak, "Scattering of Ashes Strongly Discouraged," *The Nashville Tennessean*, 3 December 1999, E1.

127:1. Ibid., 86.

128:1. Alan Wolfelt "Helping Children Understand Cremation," *The Director*, October 1999, 20.

Chapter 19: Questions about Memorialization

1. Lynch, *The Undertaking*, 117.

133:1. Jennifer Fleischner, *Mrs. Lincoln and Mrs. Keckly: The Remarkable Story of the Friendship between a First Lady and a Former Slave* (New York: Broadway Books, 2003), 237.

Chapter 20: Questions about Wills and Estates

1. Susan Stellin, "To Draft Some Wills, Computer Software Can Prove Adequate," *The Kansas City Star,* December 16, 2001, F13.

2. Joyce Madelon Winslow, "'Just Stuff?' Tell That to the Kids," *USA Today,* 19 October 2000, 27A.

3. Bill Tammeus, "Thy Will Be Done As It Is in Japan, if Not in Heaven," *The Kansas City Star,* 20 January 1997, B5.

134:1. Andrew J. Willms, "Estate-tax Relief for Owners of Family Owned Business," *The Director,* October 2000, 26.

134:2. Cited in Randy Voorhees, *Old Age Is Always 15 Years Older Than I Am* (Kansas City, Mo.: Andrews McMeel Publishing, 2001), 91.

134:3. Andy Morrison, "Where There Is a Will, There Is a Way," *Saint Luke's Hospital Foundation Traditions,* 2001, 1.

137:1. Keller and Owens Inc., "Choosing Your Executor: A Critical Estate Planning Decision," *NewsLine,* 2003, 3.

Chapter 21: Questions about Support

1. Roberts, *Death without Denial,* 78.

2. Susan Ford Wiltshire, *Seasons of Grief and Grace* (Nashville: Vanderbilt University Press, 1994), 81.

138:1. Neimeyer, *Lessons of Loss,* 96.

139:1. Barbara Bartocci, *From Hurting to Happy: Transforming Your Life after Loss* (Notre Dame, Ind.: Sorin Books, 2002), 85.

Chapter 22: Questions about Responsibility for Griever Care

1. Bartocci, *Nobody's Child Anymore,* 19.

Chapter 23: Questions about Grief in the Workplace

1. Jeffrey Zaslow, "Putting a Price Tag on Grief," *The Wall Street Journal,* 20 November 2002, D1.

2. Alice Sebold, *The Lovely Bones* (Boston: Little, Brown & Company, 2002), 159.

3. Johnette Hartnett, *Grief in the Workplace: 40 Hours Plus Overtime* (South Burlington, Vt.: Good Mourning, 1993), 8.

143:1. Russell Friedman cited in Zaslow, "Putting a Price Tag," D1, D12.
143:2. Ibid., D1.
145:1. Hartnett, *Grief in the Workplace*, 48.
145:2. Ibid., 27.

Chapter 24: Questions about Holidays and Special Days

1. Harold Ivan Smith, *The Gifts of Christmas* (Kansas City, Mo.: Beacon Hill Press, 1999), 56-57.
2. Donald L. Murray, *The Lively Shadow: Living with the Death of a Child* (New York: Ballentine, 2003), 180.
147:1. Jan Jarboe Russell, *Lady Bird: A Biography of Mrs. Johnson* (New York: Scribner, 1999), 53.
148:1. Eisenhower, *Mrs. Ike*, 173.
148:2. Alan D. Wolfelt, lecture, Olathe, Kansas, 17 February 1999.
149:1. Andersen, *Sweet Caroline*, 293.
150:1. Nancy Keller, personal correspondence, 26 August 2003.
150:2. Peter Wrench, *First Ladies: Fascinating Facts about Our Nation's First Ladies* (Dallas: Wrench Enterprises, 1996), 31.

Chapter 25: Questions about Finding Help

1. Walter, "A New Model of Grief," 11.
152:1. Harold Ivan Smith, *Death and Grief: Healing through Grief Support* (Minneapolis: Augsburg, 1995), 4.
153:1. Kushner, *The Lord Is My Shepherd*, 94-95.
156:1. Personal correspondence with the Reverend Dennis Apple, 11 September 2003.
157:1. M. J. Ryan, *The Power of Patience: How to Slow the Rush and Enjoy More Happiness, Success, and Peace Every Day* (New York: Conari Press, 2003), 3.
157:2. Parachin, *Healing Grief*, 70.

Conclusion

1. Madeleine L'Engle with Carole F. Chase, *Glimpses of Grace: Daily Thoughts and Meditations* (San Francisco: HarperSanFrancisco, 1996), 94.
2. Wolpe, *Making Loss Matter*, 5.

Other Grief Resources by Harold Ivan Smith

Grieving the Death of a Friend
176 pages, 0-8066-2842-1

Harold Ivan Smith guides the reader to move with, rather than against, the natural grief process as he explores its many aspects, including the befriending, passing, burying, mourning, remembering, and reconciling.

Grieving the Death of a Mother
144 pages, 0-8066-4347-1

Drawing on his own experience of loss as well as those of others, the author guides readers through their grief, from the process of dying through the acts of remembering and honoring a mother after her death.

On Grieving the Death of a Father
144 pages, 0-8066-2714-X

Not many books have been written to help the grieving son or daughter deal with the new reality of a deceased father. Smith has collected personal stories from well-known people to help others through their grieving process.

When Your Friend Dies
64 pages, 0-8066-4354-4

In this short volume, Harold Ivan Smith offers comfort and encouragement to those who have lost a friend by validating their grief, urging them to give their grief a voice, and remembering their friend.

Available wherever books are sold.

For information on the Association for Death Education and Counseling, please go to www.ADEC. org.